LONDON 19-7-84.

Successful investment strategy

Dedication

To my son, Simon Charles Craig, with love

Successful investment strategy

Malcolm Craig

Woodhead-Faulkner · Cambridge

Published by Woodhead-Faulkner Limited,
Fitzwilliam House, 32 Trumpington Street, Cambridge CB2 1QY, England
and
51 Washington Street, Dover, New Hampshire 03820, USA.

First published 1984

ISBN 0 85941 247 4

Library of Congress Cataloging in Publication Data

Craig, Malcolm
Successful investment strategy.
Includes Index 1. Investments 1 Title.
HG 4521.C858 1984 332.678 84–3681
ISBN 0 85941-247-4

Designed by Geoff Green

Typeset by Hands Fotoset, Leicester

Printed in Great Britain by St Edmundsbury Press, Bury St Edmunds, Suffolk

Contents

Preface

While I usually skip the Prefaces in other books, I must admit they do provide a chance to explain to the reader the rationale behind the book which follows and to provide him, or her, with guideposts.

First, my sins of omission. I had intended to include a section of the book which would show the reader how to analyse a company balance sheet, how to work out a price/earnings multiple and how to assess dividend cover. Having thought carefully about these weighty matters, I came to the conclusion that such exotica are really of little practical use to the average private investor. After all, the vast majority of readers do not have to earn their living as investment analysts. What does matter is a sense of timing when it comes to most investment sectors into which the investor puts his funds in the hope that capital gain will accrue.

On the quoted stock market – and on the Unlisted Securities Market, the Rule 163 market and the 'over-the-counter' market – the price of a share is determined by market forces. Everything known about the share is reflected in the share price, as is the investment community's expectations as to the future of the company behind the share.

I repeat, what matters is timing – getting into a share, a gilt, a unit trust or an investment trust when the unit price is low, and making one's profits when the price is high. Selling is as important as buying – a profit is never a profit unless it is taken. In order to get a sense of timing it is important to understand the background to the market in which one is operating. For this reason the first three chapters provide the background to the UK stock market and to the emergence of the 'cult of the equity' and deal with share investment in relation to inflation.

All this background is very useful but the average investor also needs to know the mechanics of the market-place in which he, or she, operates, in order to translate theory into practice – hence the rationale for chapter 4.

The book then moves on to the volatile markets which lie below the fully public stock market – in particular the Unlisted Securities Market which has enjoyed such phenomenal growth since its comparatively recent inception.

The investor in shares is also faced with a number of related opportunities. Should he 'stag' a new issue, should he take up a rights issue, should he use the options market or the traded options market and should he buy convertibles or warrants? Chapters 6 to 11 guide the reader through these share-related sections.

I have not dealt with the overseas stock markets in detail because, from practical experience, I have found that there are very few investors who invest directly into overseas markets – for one thing, it is difficult enough to monitor one's share investments in the United Kingdom. It is much more difficult for the private investor to monitor share investments made in Tokyo, Chicago, Paris or Frankfurt. Anyone seeking to invest in the Tokyo market, for example, must buy in a minimum of 1,000 share lots. There is also the difficulty of finding a broker overseas, unless one uses a London broker and faces up to paying the two sets of commission charged by the London broker and the overseas broker. The net result of this is that the majority of private investors channel their overseas investments via Britain's unit trusts and investment trusts, which are dealt with in chapters 12 and 13.

At one time – from the Victorian era, all the way through to the mid-1950s – the respectable investor avoided investment in shares as being too risky. Gilts were 'the' investment sector into which one put much of one's investment portfolio. The inflationary 1960s and 1970s caused gilts to fall into disgrace as investors watched their capital eroded as gilt prices collapsed while yields soared. However, gilts have now made a big comeback and offer many attractions to the private investor seeking income, capital gain, a combination of the two, or the recent protection provided against future inflation by index-linked gilts. All this is explained in chapters 14 and 15.

There is a natural progression from gilts to the insurance-linked bond market – which rivals the unit trust market in size – and then to the Eurobond market. Little has been written about this vast and volatile market for United Kingdom investors for the simple reason that they were unable, until October 1979 when exchange controls were lifted, to buy Eurobonds, or the zero coupon and deep discount bonds. These are even more recent phenomena on the investment scene and are of particular interest to those seeking to diversify part of their investment portfolio outside the United Kingdom and outside sterling.

This brings me to the importance of every investor keeping a 'cash cushion' of 10, or 20, per cent of his portfolio in sectors which will pay him the highest return and which will return the cash to him quickly. Chapter 19 deals with putting one's surplus cash to best use in the sterling money funds which were introduced in the 1970s. Chapter 20 deals with more recent investments – the offshore currency funds which provided 'roll up' facilities ('rolling up' income into capital gain) and foreign currency deposits.

In chapter 21 I deal with the most speculative investment – the commodity investment, whether direct, or via the onshore and offshore commodity funds. I trust that I have highlighted sufficiently the pitfalls which lie in wait for the unwary in this largely unregulated sector.

No book on investment would be complete without a mention of gold. As mentioned earlier, it is advisable for the investor to keep 10 per cent of his portfolio in cash as a 'cash cushion'. It makes equal sense for him to keep a further 10 per cent in gold, or gold coins. Anyone who followed this philosophy during the years of hyper-inflation in Western Europe in the 1920s (particularly if they were Jewish and lived in Germany) will endorse this. Chapters 22 to 24 provide detailed guidance on investment in gold.

Last, but not least, all too few investors think of their pension as an investment. With the enormous assistance provided by the Inland Revenue, pensions are one of the best investments of all, which is why I end with a chapter on the subject.

Successful investment strategy covers the years from 1950 to 1983.

M.C.
December 1983

1

Ordinary shares – the lessons of history

One reason for investing in shares is the potential reward to be gained – the reward which may be reaped from buying shares in a company which goes on to make higher profits in which the shareholders participate by way of increasing dividends, allied with capital gain from the consequent increase in the share price. The rationale for investing in shares is that the investor can not only get income in the form of dividends, but also gets the opportunity to make capital gains, as share prices should theoretically outpace the rate of inflation and thus maintain the real value of the investor's capital as well as increase his capital sum. Two very comfortable reasons – and if share investment worked like this in practice there would be many more contented investors around.

In reality share investment, like the curate's egg, 'is good in parts'. (You will recall the apocryphal story of the bishop's wife entertaining the young curate at breakfast and asking him about the state of his boiled egg. Searching around for a diplomatic answer, he came up with the best he could think of – 'it's good in parts'.) The same answer holds equally true for investment in shares, which is why it is as well to follow a strategy which scoops out the good parts of the egg and avoids the bad.

Risk and reward

The essential fact to bear in mind about share investment, whether over the short, or long, term, is that it is a risk investment sector. The reason why it can be worth taking the risk as an investor is because, in an inflationary era, the real value of capital is eroded steadily.

The erosive effects of inflation

As you can see from Table 1 (which charts the changing value of the pound since 1825) the economist's point about money being a medium of exchange, i.e. having a price which is established by demand and supply, is graphically illustrated.

Table 1 Purchasing power of the pound (1914=100p)

1825	65.08	1865	83.75	1904	121.66	1945	—
6	75.04	6	83.75	5	118.33	6	37.91
7	75.04	7	85.04	6	110.00	7	35.04
8	83.75	8	85.08	7	105.00	8	32.91
9	85.04	9	86.25	8	116.25	9	32.08
				9	112.08		
1830	83.75	1870	88.75	1910	108.75	1950	31.25
1	82.50	1	85.04	1	105.00	1	28.75
2	87.08	2	78.75	2	100.00	2	27.08
3	90.08	3	76.66	3	100.00	3	26.66
4	87.08	4	82.91	4	100.00	4	26.25
5	85.00	5	88.75	5	81.25	5	25.04
6	73.75	6	89.16	6	68.33	6	24.16
7	80.08	7	90.04	7	56.66	7	23.33
8	80.08	8	97.50	8	44.16	8	22.91
9	76.66	9	102.50	9	46.66	9	22.91
1840	77.91	1880	96.25	1920	40.00	1960	22.50
1	79.16	1	100.00	1	44.16	1	22.08
2	90.04	2	100.08	2	54.58	2	21.25
3	96.25	3	103.33	3	57.50	3	20.08
4	98.33	4	112.08	4	57.08	4	20.04
5	92.50	5	118.33	5	56.66	5	19.58
6	92.50	6	122.50	6	58.33	6	18.75
7	87.08	7	124.16	7	59.58	7	18.33
8	100.00	8	121.66	8	60.04	8	17.50
9	105.00	9	118.33	9	60.08	9	16.25
1850	105.00	1890	118.33	1930	63.33	1970	15.83
1	102.50	1	118.33	1	67.91	1	14.58
2	105.00	2	124.58	2	69.58	2	13.33
3	92.50	3	124.58	3	71.25	3	12.29
4	82.50	4	135.00	4	70.08	4	11.25
5	85.04	5	135.00	5	70.00	5	9.37
6	82.50	6	140.00	6	67.91	6	8.33
7	79.16	7	135.00	7	65.00	7	5.90
8	88.75	8	133.33	8	64.16	8	5.83
9	88.33	9	124.58	9	—	9	5.62
1860	85.04	1900	112.91	1940	—	1980	4.58
1	86.25	1	121.66	1	—	1	4.16
2	83.75	2	122.50	2	—	2	3.54
3	82.50	3	122.50	3	—		
4	80.08			4	—		

Compiled by E. Barry Bowyer.

Taking 1914 as his benchmark (with £1 equalling the index figure of 100), E. Barry Bowyer has traced the fluctuating fortunes of the pound, in terms of its purchasing power, back to 1825 when the index figure was only 65.08.

If you had had money, the year in which it would have bought you the most was 1896. This was the heyday of Victorian mercantile and manufacturing strength when there was also plenty of low cost labour. In that year the index reached 140. Since then it has gone down, falling steeply during the First World War and its aftermath. This was followed by a recovery during the Great Depression of the 1930s when the pound struggled back to an index figure of 71.25 in 1933. This struggle – similar to the one in the early 1980s – gave rise, in some quarters, to a belief that you can only have 'sound money' during a depression.

The Second World War and the years thereafter witnessed a big drop in the purchasing power of the pound from 64.16 in 1938 to 37.91 in 1946. The post-war years have never seen the purchasing power of the pound stop falling, particularly during the 1970s when the pound's value slid, at ever-increasing speeds, towards the abyss of hyper-inflation. At the time of writing, the index figure for the pound is 3.54 – having been ten times that figure in 1947. Any investor who locked up money in fixed-interest investments, such as gilts, or left cash in a bank or building society deposit will, by now, have seen the real value of his capital almost extinguished.

With money losing its value so quickly, those with capital at risk seek to preserve the real value of that capital in order to protect themselves and their families. On the other hand, anyone with debts to pay off – such as a house mortgage – benefits from the fact that the real value of these goes down as money loses its value. Anyone raising a mortgage of, say, £10,000 back in 1970 – which may have seemed a very large mortgage at the time – would have been complacently slapping himself on the back ten years later after witnessing a decade of high inflation and big jumps in house prices. One reaction to the value of money going down resulted in the *cult of the equity*.

2

The 'cult of the equity'

The 'cult of the equity' was when both private and institutional investors alike started to invest more heavily in ordinary shares from the mid-1950s onwards. The cult of the equity can be seen from Fig. 1 which also shows the rate of inflation over a 50-year period.

Until the mid-1950s 'respectable' investors were much more interested in low-risk investments, such as Government gilts, than they were in investment in ordinary shares. Although it is an extreme, and fictional, case, the way in which the ultra-cautious Timothy Forsyte invested the sale proceeds of his publishing company in Government gilt-edged stock for an exceedingly low yield (graphically described in John Galsworthy's *Forsyte Saga)* typifies the nineteenth century approach to investment.

Indeed, this school of thought was also typical of the twentieth century investor until well after the Second World War. A modest holding of 'blue-chip' shares – in leading industrial and manufacturing companies – was certainly a respectable strategy to pursue. However, the conservative investor kept the bulk of his capital in copper-bottomed investments, such as land, or in Government gilt-edged stock. It was the Church Commissioners – or rather the committee which looked after the Church of England's finances – who first saw the possibilities offered by ordinary shares as a means of maintaining and increasing the real value of the capital under their management, as opposed to investing in fixed-interest securities.

The stampede of the wealthier British investors to purchase ordinary shares was given an added fillip by the fact that for much of the 1950s and 1960s there was no capital gains tax. During an era in which income tax rates were to rise to very punishing levels indeed, the lack of any tax on capital gains made on share dealing was a strong motivator to invest in shares.

The flood of private investment funds was increased by the flow of cash pouring, week by week, into the hands of institutional fund managers in the City. The latter, comprising a select band of sober individuals, look after the investment strategy of company pension funds, deploy the assets of insurance companies and carry out similar tasks for a host of other financial institutions. Steadily, the British became more insurance, and pension, conscious, while the unit trust movement developed at the same time. Both the private investor and the fund managers – the latter were to come to dominate the stock market completely in due course owing to the very weight of cash at their command – were prepared to accept a lower income, in the form of a dividend, from their ordinary shareholdings than could be obtained from medium- and long-term Government stocks.

The reverse yield gap

The fact that they were prepared to take this lower income, despite the

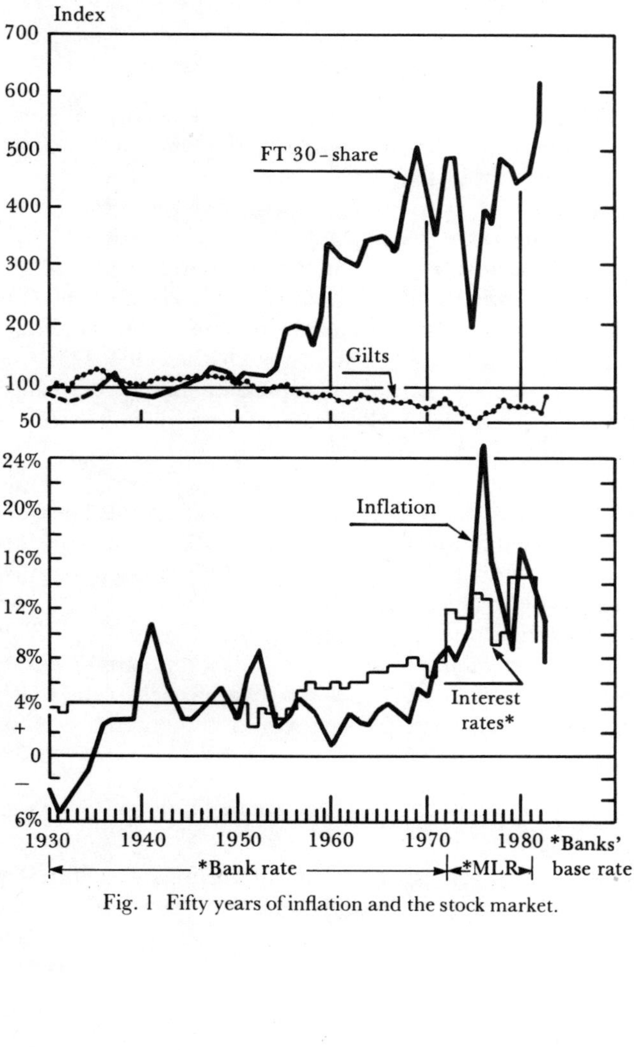

Fig. 1 Fifty years of inflation and the stock market.

knowledge that they were investing in a risky area – shares as opposed to (theoretically) risk-free Government gilts – resulted in a new piece of jargon. This change in investment psychology was called the 'reverse yield gap' by operators in the market. This was the difference between the yield on undated gilts and the yield on ordinary shares. The pressure of share buying forced down the yield on ordinary shares as companies no longer had to produce dividends in excess of the yields on Government stocks in order to attract investment money. Lack of demand for gilts forced the yields up over the dividend levels on ordinary shares as the Government had to tempt buyers by offering higher, and still higher, interest coupons on gilt offerings which were needed to meet the Government's borrowing requirement in the era of a Welfare State. During the 1970s' waves of hyper-inflation which hit Britain the interest rates on gilts were driven still higher in order to compensate investors for the fall in the value of money, both actual and prospective.

Shares outpace inflation – in theory

The reasoning behind taking refuge – and making capital gains – from ordinary shares was that the shareholder had a stake in a company which manufactured products or made available services. Such companies could increase the prices of their goods in line with their own costs (or at an even faster pace) and thus keep up with, or outdistance, inflation. So the investor was rewarded, not only by a dividend from the company's ability to produce increased profits, and thereby pay dividends, but also as a result of the increase in the value of the shares as companies ploughed back profits into producing more goods, and services, while the value of the companies' assets also rose at the same rate as inflation. The shareholder had a stake in something which could keep its head above water during an era of erosive inflation.

The buyer of a long-term bond, or a long-term Government gilt, was, it was felt, on a hiding to nothing as the interest rate on his bond or gilt was fixed, and therefore did not keep pace with inflation, which meant that the capital value of the amount he had invested in buying bonds or gilts (or kept in a bank, or building society, deposit account) was steadily destroyed.

Anyone who bought, say, 2½ per cent Consols in the early 1960s at over £50 per £100 nominal would have lost the bulk of his capital investment by 1974 when the price of undated gilts nearly approached their yields. (For example, a gilt yielding 17½ per cent could be bought for £18 per £100 nominal at the time.)

The end of the 'cult of the equity'

The 'cult of the equity' lasted until the vicious bear market of 1974 when the *Financial Times* 30 share index dropped to 149.6 (on 3 January 1975, to be precise) from its previous 'high' of 542 reached in the spring of 1972. There were numerous reasons why the 'cult of the equity' came to an end. However, the immediate causes were twofold.

One cause was the quadrupling of the OPEC oil prices in the early 1970s. This struck the oil-seeking industrialised world (which had long been accustomed to relatively cheap oil imports) like a sledgehammer, and led it into an economic recession.

The other cause was the default by the West German bank, Herstatt, which took place at much the same time. Rather like a pebble dropped into a pool, the crisis of confidence 'ripples' from the Herstatt collapse led to an overall lack of confidence in the UK banking structure. The final straw – which almost collapsed confidence in the UK financial system altogether – was the default of many of the secondary banks in the UK as a result of the over-inflated property price 'balloon'. This 'balloon' had been the creation of too much easy money, allied with a stupendous rise in house, and commercial, property prices in 1970–73. The secondary banks – and many first-line banks – were all caught by the property price collapse because high interest charges could no longer be paid by the borrowers. They had been chanelling money into the hands of property developers and they were willing to lend 100 per cent, or even 110 per cent, of the property developers' financial requirements. The undermining of confidence resulting from the Herstatt affair and the collapse in property prices percolated through to the British banking system. The whole basis of banking rests on an air of confidence. The loss of the latter resulted in the collapse of the secondary banks and the launch of the Bank of England 'lifeboat' to ensure that the collapse would at least be orderly. As Sir Kenneth Cork, the leading company liquidator at that time (who advised the Bank of England during the 1973–74 period) pointed out later, if £100 million worth of property is unloaded on to the market all in one go there will be a dearth of buyers. However, if only £1 million worth of property is unloaded on to the market, some measure of confidence can be maintained and buyers can be found.

So great was the loss of confidence at the time that even the National Westminster Bank was affected by rumours as to its financial soundness, causing it one Friday evening in 1975 to rush out a press statement to the effect that there was no cause for concern.

Exploding a fallacy

Against a backdrop of collapsing confidence in the very fabric of the Western monetary system, private investors and institutional fund managers were becoming aware of other fallacies concerning the 'cult of the equity'. One was the concept that a company could always protect its shareholders by passing on, in the form of increasing dividends, the benefits from the rising prices charged for the goods and services which the company made and provided. This fallacy was exploded when dividend restraints and price curbs were introduced, along with attempts to limit incomes.

Another problem, of which shareholders were abruptly made aware, was that, when companies hit flat demand – or demand is reduced, resulting in lower turnover, reduced profits and even losses – the dividend could be cut or even omitted altogether. The Victorian awareness of the risk of share investment returned with a vengeance.

Yet another area for concern was the realisation of the power of the trades unions – particularly the strong unions – which could halt the economy entirely. The most telling example of this power was the destruction of the Heath Government by the National Union of Miners, after Edward Heath decided to go to the polls on a 'who runs the country' platform after months of electricity cuts.

In that miserable winter of 1974 stockbrokers laid off staff in their hundreds, and those who were left spoke of the merit of investing gold coins (which reached the high price of $197.50 per ounce of gold on the last trading day of 1974), silver bullion, or anything which might survive as a store of value as the Apocalypse approached. Like all things to do with share investment – which manifests an aspect of human behaviour primarily impelled by greed and fear, and without much in the way of apparent logic to it – the slide was overdone.

3

Shares and inflation

A measure of recovery

A few astute investment managers started buying shares cheaply in January 1975 when Britain's (then) best blue-chip share, ICI, was yielding a good 14.6 per cent. Other professionals (investment managers with mountains of cash sitting on the money markets) were anxious not to be left behind. In one heady day in February 1975 the *Financial Times* 30 share index leapt nearly 20 points, and from a low of 146 reached 300 inside three months. By 14 September 1977 the index reached 549.2, making up the losses sustained between 1972 and 1974. (Figure 2 illustrates these rises.)

Since then, the *Financial Times* index has really lost ground if measured in real terms, after adjusting for inflation. True, it went on to exceed the 800 mark in 1984, but even at this level, once the increase is adjusted for the fall in the purchasing power of money, the index of 30 shares which the *Financial Times* uses as a rough and ready measure to the behaviour of the stock market, is not appreciably above the level it reached after Dunkirk – its all-time low point. Once inflation is taken into account, the *FT* 30 share index should have been comfortably at the 2,100 mark by 1984 in order to maintain its level in real terms throughout its long life.

Another fallacy which has been shown up is that, far from performing well during inflationary times, as you can see from Fig. 3, the value of shares actually plunged in times of high inflation. The main reason for this apparent contradiction is that, in times of inflation, the cost of money – the rate of interest charged on bank overdrafts and term loans – rises until a company is shouldering a sometimes unacceptably high burden of debt. The cost of labour also goes up during inflationary times, unless there is a wages and incomes freeze, or at least a limitation on wages growth. Yet another cost is the rise in price of raw materials. Unless prices at which companies sell their goods and services can be adjusted accordingly – which

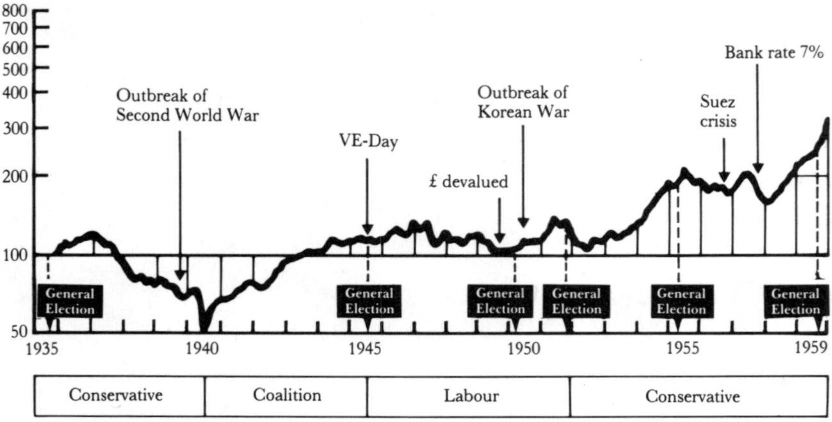

Fig. 2 *Financial Times* Industrial Ordinary Index (courtesy of the *Financial Times*).

is difficult if prices are also held under constraint – then profits suffer.

The combined effects of high interest cost burdens, high costs of labour and raw materials allied with the savage recession in 1981, 1982 and 1983, resulted in record numbers of company bankruptcies and the launching of a 'lifeboat mark II' by the banking system to help some of Britain's biggest companies. Instead of making automatic increases in sales and profits, companies found they were facing sharp drops in sales and profits, and faced the bleak prospect, or the actuality, of losses. Cost cutting became the order of the day, and the biggest cost – labour – produced the longest dole queues seen since the 'Hungry '30s'.

While a bull market mentality was still holding good in 1982, 1983 and 1984, the market itself became, in essence, a two-tier market. The upper 'bull' tier was made up from high flying shares in areas such as money broking – for example, the Exco International new issue in 1981 was a massive 62½ times oversubscribed. More money was put up for a handful of brokers wheeling and dealing in currencies in markets round the world than the entire market capitalisation of one of the British Clearing Banks with all its high street branches, long history and host of subsidiaries. The lower 'bear' tier was made up of the solid manufacturing companies which had been hardest hit by the recession – the Turner & Newall's and the rest, about whose prospects the stock market took a distinctly jaundiced viewpoint.

Shares do not benefit from inflation. Figure 4 shows the state of the UK stock market since 1967 – as illustrated by the movements of the *Financial Times* 30 share index, and by a better market barometer, the *Financial Times* Actuaries All-Share index. If one takes a 50-year view, the London bear market of 1974 and 1975 (so graphically shown in Fig. 4) looks like only a minor interruption of a sustained long-term bull trend. It is reasonably

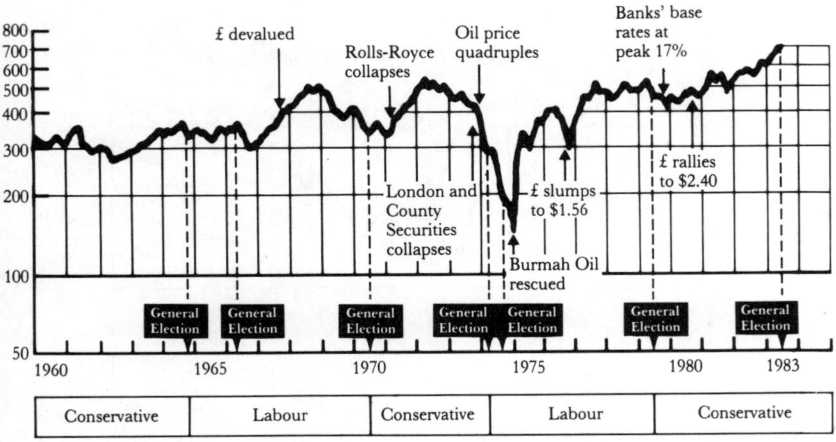

plain to see that the market has moved very strongly in reaction to movements in inflation – which is a most potent factor to bear in mind for the investment strategist.

The stock market was very firm in the 1950s and 1960s when inflation was low. When inflation rises to unacceptable levels – as was the case in 1973 and 1974 – the market weakens. It is something of a contradiction in logic in that shares should protect the investor against inflation because the companies in which the shares are bought should be able to put up prices for goods and services in line with inflation. The trouble is that high rates of inflation bring with them high interest rates with which to protect the pound. Inflation brings with it unemployment as Governments fight to restore sound money – the main platform of the Thatcherite Government. Unemployment reduces demand for goods and services and the end result is a recession.

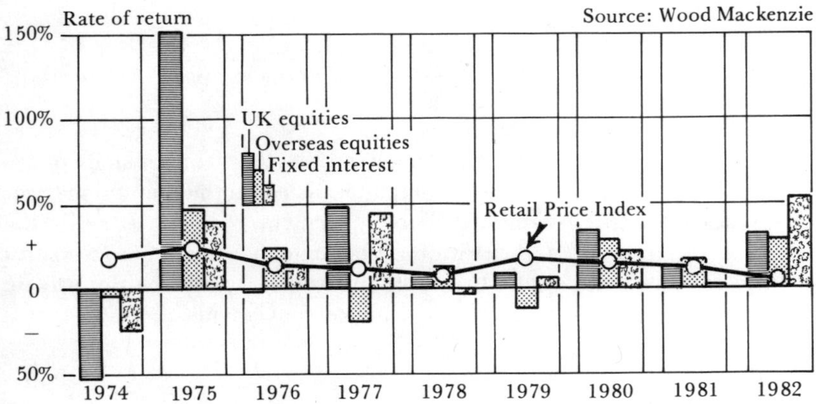

Fig. 3 Equities and inflation.

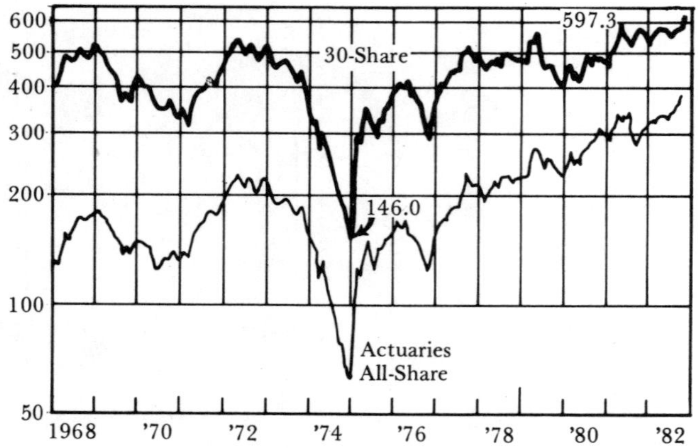

Fig. 4 The *Financial Times* Indices (courtesy of the *Financial Times*).

The FT *30 share index – a note*

While the *Financial Times* 30 share index is a good measure of short-term trends in the stock market, its method of construction has the effect of introducing a downward bias which can be quite serious on a timescale of several decades. It is therefore best to view the numerical landmarks shown in Fig. 4 as statistical events rather than as key indicators of economic or political development.

The *FT* 30 share index is over 48 years old and many of the original companies – such as Austin Motor, Rolls-Royce, United Steel and Bolsover Colliery – have met with reverses, nationalisation or even collapse. However, 12 of the constituent companies have survived in much the same form to the present day. The index touched an all-time low of 49.4 at the time of Dunkirk. Its true all-time high point was 521.9, reached in September 1968.

The FT/*Stock Exchange 100 share index – a new index*

A new index of share movement – the *FT*/Stock Exchange 100 share index (known as 'footsie') was introduced in 1984. Based on the share prices of the 100 most highly capitalised companies listed on the London market, it provides a minute-by-minute share movement monitor. LIFFE (the London International Finance Futures Exchange) has introduced a futures contract based on this index to enable institutional and wealthy private investors to hedge against future stock market movements.

4

The mechanics of the market-place

Buying shares

On the whole, the small investor gets a pretty raw deal when it comes to buying and selling shares. The majority of stockbrokers prefer institutional investment business – although provincial brokers are more geared up to serve private clients (and don't have to pay the high rent and rates of the City of London). Costs for buying shares in small amounts can be prohibitive, as you can see from Table 2.

Table 2 Typical costs of buying shares

	500 shares at £1	1,500 shares at £1
Investor puts in	£500	£1,500
On top of this his costs are:	£	£
Broker's commission (approx.)	15	24.75
Stamp duty (2 per cent)	10	30
Contract stamp	0.10	0.60
VAT	2.25	3.72
Total	£527.35	£1,559.07
Costs as percentage	5½ per cent	3.9 per cent

When it comes to selling shares, no stamp duty is payable, but the other costs are the same as the costs listed in Table 2 – although some brokers charge less for selling. Typical expenses on selling 500 shares at £1 apiece are 3.5 per cent or 1.9 per cent on 1,500 shares.

As you can see, the capital appreciation you have to get on a small share purchase has to be over 10 per cent – just to cover costs. For the bigger investor, once he, or she, has a capital sum of £20,000 to £25,000 plus to invest, the brokers will offer a discretionary management service – meaning that they will take buying and selling decisions on your behalf. Some brokers offer such a management service and content themselves with the commission generated by handling the portfolio; others charge a fee. If a client prefers a non-discretionary arrangement (which means the broker handling his, or her, account has to go back to the client to take instructions regarding buying and selling shares) a higher fee can be charged for the work involved. Once an investor has a share portfolio of over £50,000 he becomes of interest to the merchant bank investment departments who will manage the portfolio for him, for a fee based on the value of the funds under management. Some merchant banks have much higher minimum cut off points – £100,000 per portfolio, £500,000 or even £1 million.

Of course, the small investor can use a bank or a broker as long as he is willing to make his own buying and selling decisions. There is no difference in cost in using a bank, except in the case of Barclays which charges a flat fee of £5 plus VAT for carrying out share dealings on behalf of their customers in addition to the other commissions payable. Banks route a buying, or selling, order to the bank's own stockbroker and get return commission from the broker. Orders placed through a bank tend to be slower in being put through – in view of the need to route the order via the broker – and can be more costly because a broker may not feel himself under any obligation to beat down the jobber's spread (profit) quoted for a small deal, and therefore will pay the top price for the share.

Alternatively the investor can write to The Stock Exchange, London EC2 (telephone number: 01-588 2355) and ask for a list of brokers interested in taking on further private client business. If you live outside London you will get a full list of regional brokers sent to you; if you live inside London you get a list of three brokers. When approaching a broker (if you are a small investor) the first question you should ask is: 'What is your minimum commission?' Despite The Stock Exchange commission scales, all brokers charge minimum commissions on small deals, and this can vary from £7, charged by a provincial broker, to, typically, £15 by a City of London broker. Once you appoint a broker, the latter will check out your credit-worthiness by taking up bank references and consulting The Stock Exchange Mutual Reference List. There is also believed to be an informal blacklist circulating among the brokers. Once you decide to buy, you will receive a contract note from the broker within a few days which details the shares bought and the price and the costs involved, and he will give you the 'settlement date' by which you have to pay (usually within two weeks of the deal). Bear in mind that you have to pay the 'jobber's turn' of a minimum of 1 per cent – but it can be larger – which must be added to your costs.

Bed and breakfasting

The old style 'bed and breakfasting' was designed for the investor who sought to make a profit just before the end of a tax year and continue holding his shares. It involved an overnight sale and re-purchase arrangement of the shares with the connivance of the jobber who took, perhaps, a ½p 'turn' per share on the transaction. This left the investor in the happy position of taking a profit up to his tax exempt allowance and continuing to hold the share.

This was killed off in the Finance Act 1982. However, it is still possible to 'bed and breakfast' for 'cash settlement' using the facility already employed by The Stock Exchange for gilts trading, new issues and rights. Deals for cash are settled on the second business day following the transaction. If the sale and subsequent repurchase are effected on consecutive days, then settlement will also be on consecutive days. Provided the settlement dates of the two transactions are different, the Inland Revenue will identify the sale with the original purchase, leaving the new purchase price to apply for the purpose of any future transactions in the share. Since the two transactions take place within the same account period there is only one lot of broker's commission to pay, but you cannot avoid stamp duty or paying the full jobber's turn. Any evidence of special terms on the sale or repurchase price will be seized on by the Inland Revenue. All the formalities of settlement must be observed.

Investors should lodge their share certificates with their broker ahead of the transaction so that he can deliver the stock physically to the market when he sells. The investor should also instruct his broker, in writing, to deal for cash settlement and it can be useful to have a letter back for the broker (dated on the day the purchase is effected) saying 'the shares have today been purchased, for cash, in accordance with your instructions on the telephone this morning'. If you have some shares which cost you a fraction of their current value you may be able to kill two birds with one stone – using up your annual capital gains tax allowance by selling and repurchasing part of the hold and simultaneously lifting the cost of those shares for subsequent indexation (providing you hold onto them for a year or more).

A note on capital gains tax

One reason why the UK stock market had a long bull phase from 1975 onwards was the steady lowering of the tax on capital gains. As the tax on capital gains is 30 per cent, there is a reasonably generous yearly exemption of £5,300, under which level no capital gains tax is charged at all, and, in arriving at this figure, off-setting capital losses can be taken into account. once a share is held for over one year, the gains are reduced by the indexation allowance which is established by the increase in the retail price index. Ignoring, for the moment, the yearly capital gains tax-free allowance, and any offsetting losses, take the case, set out in Table 3, of a portfolio of shares bought back in April 1965 for £12,076 and sold in April 1983 for £28,555.

The actual gain would have been reduced by the exempt allowance of

Table 3 Indexation – a worked example

	£
Sale proceeds of shares	28,555
Value of purchase at 6 April 1965	12,076
Indexation allowance at 4 per cent	484
	12,560
Chargeable gain	£15,995

£5,000 in 1982–83, so capital gains tax would be chargeable at 30 per cent on £10,995 (£15,995 minus the £5,000 exemption).

Capital gains tax – the history

Capital gains tax was first introduced by the Macmillan Government in April 1962. The first CGT was on the sale of assets which had been held for six months only – the idea being to tax investors who bought and sold shares quickly. In 1965 a CGT of one third – to be charged on the sale of anything from private possessions to stocks and shares – was introduced.

Successive Finance Acts since 1965 have raised the threshold at which CGT becomes payable, but only the Finance Acts of 1980 and 1982 made an appreciable difference, raising the threshold to £3,000 and £5,000 and the 1983 Budget raised this to £5,300. Indexation was introduced in 1982. This means that an investor, when arriving at the capital gains tax liability with investments held for over one year, can reduce the taxable gain in line with the retail price increase over the tax year. One result of CGT is that investment in owner-occupied property has been the only investment with which to make a tax-free capital gain – a potent factor in property prices soaring.

Who's who in the stockbroker league

Private investors need advice as to which stockbrokers to use. Here is a list of top brokers, drawn up by the leading fund investors in the land.

- James Capel
- Scrimgeour, Kemp-Gee
- Phillips & Drew
- Laing & Cruickshank
- Wood Mackenzie
- Hoare Govett
- W. Greenwell
- De Zoete & Bevan
- Simon & Coates
- Rowe & Pitman

These are all large firms accustomed to providing services for clients from the large institutions – they all have limits as to the size of the private client they take on. Top specialists in each stock market sector are given in Table 4.

Table 4 The top specialists in each stock market sector

Electricals:	Scrimgeour Kemp-Gee, The Stock Exchange. (Tel: 01-638 6070.)
Electronics, Radio/TV:	(As above.)
Wines and spirits:	Wood Mackenzie, 62 Threadneedle Street, London EC2. (Tel: 01-600 3600.)
Tobacco:	De Zoete & Bevan, 25 Finsbury Circus, London EC2. (Tel: 01-588 4141.)
Food retailing:	Scrimgeour, Kemp-Gee. (Address as before.)
Stores:	(As above.)
Industrial holding companies:	Hoare Govett, Heron House, 319 High Holborn, London WC1. (Tel: 01-242 2848.)
Office equipment:	Scott Goff Hancock, Salisbury House, London Wall, London EC2. (Tel: 01-628 4433.)
Oils:	Wood Mackenzie. (Address as before.)
Merchant banks and issuing houses:	Laing & Cruickshank The Stock Exchange, London EC2. (Tel: 01-588 2800.)
Hire purchase:	Laing & Cruickshank (Address as before.)
Property:	Rowe & Pitman, City Gate House, Finsbury Square, London EC2. (Tel: 01-606 1066.)
Gold:	James Capel, 100 Old Broad Street, London EC2. (Tel: 01-588 6010.)
Mining finance:	James Capel. (Address as above.)
Gilt-edged securities:	Greenwell, Bow Bells House, Bread Street, London EC4. (Tel: 01-236 2040.)
Equity markets:	Phillips & Drew, 120 Moorgate, London EC2N 6XP. (Tel: 01-628 4444.)
General economic forecasting:	Phillips & Drew. (Address as above.)

5

Three alternative markets

There is a choice of three additional markets run by The Stock Exchange for trading in shares. These include the market in shares run by licensed dealers in securities, and by stockbrokers, and the Unlisted Securities Market (USM) in which brokers, merchant banks and licensed dealers are all involved, and the 'over-the-counter' markets run by Granville and Co., a licensed dealer in securities, and other licensed dealers.

The stock market itself is the market in which institutions and private investors can buy and sell 'fully listed' shares (there are 2,728 companies with a full Stock Exchange listing), whether your taste runs to the blue-blooded (or at least blue-chip) giants such as Unilever, ICI or Marks & Spencer, or to those little-known companies which investment analysts love to hunt with enthusiasm. All these companies, the mighty and the midget alike, have to abide by the strict rules and regulations governing the conduct of a public quoted company.

Rule 163

Of the many Stock Exchange rules, Rule 163 is the one you most frequently hear about. Under this rule stockbrokers have been allowed to deal in shares, subject to prior Stock Exchange approval. Rule 163 was really designed for occasional deals in football club shares and the like, or to establish an arm's-length valuation of private company shares held in a deceased estate. The trouble here was that enterprising companies spotted the attractions of this little-regulated twilight zone. It offered the virtues of tradability, along with a low cost and perfunctory requirements for disclosure of company information. Companies listed under Rule 163 include Weetabix, the entrepreneurial Hesketh motorcycles, which later went into liquidation, and Camra (Real Ale) Investments.

Independent oil exploration companies, operating onshore and offshore, which lacked the necessary five-year profit record to gain access to the capital (needed for drilling for oil and gas) from the fully public market were able to obtain this through Rule 163. Under this could be found Aran Energy, Berkeley Exploration & Production, Cluff Oil and Sovereign Oil and Gas.

The Stock Exchange decided to stop this fairly loose and unregulated market from booming even further in order to prevent any risk of future scandal if a company listed under Rule 163 was to go bust, casting doubts on the Stock Exchange's ability to police share dealings. The Unlisted Securities Market was therefore established.

The Unlisted Securities Market

The Unlisted Securities Market deals with nearly 200 companies' shares. (The name is something of a nonsense, incidentally; 'lists' abound of the companies so far 'listed' on the USM, which started in November 1980.)

Companies seeking an USM quotation have to meet two basic criteria. First, the company must be registered as a public listed company under the Companies Act 1980. Secondly it must have some sort of track record – normally a minimum of three years' trading.

This second criterion can be waived if a company is involved in high technology work, such as Bio-Isolates (Holdings), and can demonstrate the commercial value of its research in a prospectus. Oil exploration companies registered in the UK or Eire, too, can be admitted to the USM without a three-year trading record.

For a company to enter the USM, it has to make available at least 10 per cent of its company's issued share capital (compared, with a minimum of 25 per cent if a company is going fully public). Normally this 10 per cent (or 15, 20 or 30 per cent) will be 'placed' on the market by a merchant bank or a stockbroker. They will buy up the shares and place them at a higher price around their clients. Occasionally the shares will be issued by way of an offer by tender, or will merely be introduced to the market.

The upper ceiling on a placing is £3 million and the total market capitalisation of a company placing its shares on the USM must not exceed £15 million. If it is more than £15 million, or if the company wants to raise more than £3 million, then it has to make an 'offer for sale'. Under this system the merchant bank or broker again buys up the shares, but then invites institutional and private investors to apply for them at a fixed price.

To make sure, on a placing, that the whole deal isn't kept cosily in a narrow, incestuous circle, a quarter of the shares being placed must be made available to the stockjobbers. This is so that any member of the investing public who wants to buy the shares can do so.

Prescribed format laid down

When a company applies for admission to the USM, it has to prepare its particulars for the Extel Unlisted Securities Market Service and it has to follow a prescribed format laid down by The Stock Exchange. If, on entry to the USM, the company's shareholders want to sell some of their own shares immediately – rather than merely being 'introduced' to the market and sitting tight – then a prospectus (including an accountant's report) is essential. This prospectus also forms the Extel Card with a few minor additions.

If the company wants to be 'introduced' to the market, and the shareholders don't want to sell shares, the company doesn't have to produce an accountant's report. Instead it produces a substitute – a table of financial statistics covering the past five years' trading, or for shorter periods if it hasn't been trading that long.

Once a company joins the USM, the directors have to sign a 'general undertaking' which ensures that they continue to disclose enough information so that shareholders and potential shareholders can form an accurate view of how the company is doing. It all helps to avoid creating a false market in the shares. One other point – the company has to make known its entry to the USM by means of an advertisement in at least one leading daily newspaper and, if the company enters the USM via an 'offer for sale', the advertisement has to contain a summary of the terms of the offer.

The role of the sponsor

The company can't do any of this without a sponsor – normally a merchant bank or a stockbroker. It also has to appoint a stockbroker as the company's official broker. Since most companies entering the USM are on the small side, and use the 'placing' route rather than the 'offer for sale' route, it is easier (and cheaper) to use a broker than a merchant bank, that is unless the issue is a big one, and the company needs bridging finance from a merchant bank, pending the flotation.

The broker carries out a detailed examination of the company and assesses it against its industrial sector's background in order to become familiar with its history, market and sales structure, its management, labour force and finances. If the broker thinks that the USM is not suitable for the company and decides it could do better with a term loan from one of the banks then he will say so.

If he decides that the USM is the right avenue for the company to take, he prepares a proposal for the company, detailing the recommended mechanics of flotation, the timetable, the type of issue and the terms at which the issue could be made. If necessary, a capital re-organisation will be made to weed out 'founders' shares' and 'A' non-voting shares. These are not suitable when the company is moving to public company status by an issue of shares on the USM.

The actual timetable for a USM flotation would take from, say, 1 January to mid-March. The pricing of the shares to be issued would be left until the very last moment. The broker has the vital job of pricing the shares. His ability to do it correctly comes from his knowledge and experience of the requirements of potential investors in the new issue market, and from day-to-day monitoring and assessment of the market rating which the shares of similar companies are already getting in the market.

Once a company is launched, dealing in the shares on the USM is no different from dealing in publicly-quoted companies. For the investor, commissions on share dealing are the same and stockbrokers' dealing and settlement procedures are just as strictly regulated. Investors in USM shares are also protected under the Stock Exchange Compensation Fund on the same terms as investors in the shares of fully public companies.

The total bill for a £500,000 placing on the USM would, broadly speaking, be around the £50,000 mark, or half what is needed for a similar placing on the main Stock Exchange.

The 'over-the-counter' market (OTC)

Granville and Co. is the biggest of the OTC dealers, having been set up by an American, M. J. Nightingale, on the lines of the United States' 'over-the-counter' market. Granville and Co. (the firm changed its name after the departure of Nightingale) aims to provide an American investment bank range of services to its clients and has been running this market on these lines since 1972. Granville's main aim is to look after its clients rather than create an active market – as a result, it does not welcome speculative investors but prefers institutional investment clients. It is the antithesis of the markets operated by the other licensed dealers.

Other firms in this sector welcome speculative investors. One of the best known is Harvard Securities. A typical share handled by Harvard is VTC which acquires the rights to video films and then markets video tapes. When it needed funds, Harvard arranged a £1 million placing in 1983. Since companies of this type, seeking to broaden the market in their shares by means of the OTC market, often have only a short trading record, Harvard looks closely at the management of the potential OTC company, and at its product, before getting involved. For example, Taddale Investments, a finance and investment group, raised £2 million via Harvard when its original shareholders, who wanted to realise their profits, placed part of their equity on the over-the-counter market.

If the Unlisted Securities Market can be likened to a nursery slope, the share market 'below' the USM can be likened to a crêche. This is a somewhat shadowy market in shares which is referred to, variously, as the 'over-the-counter' market, and the Rule 163 market. The two merge into each other because, in both cases, share dealings are carried out in the shares of a reasonably small group of companies.

Take the market sector referred to as the 'over-the-counter' market – a market which is very big in the USA but one which has developed within a system of statutory regulation which is not duplicated in the UK. Some 30 shares are traded in this fragmented market by licensed dealers such as Granville and Co., Harvard Securities and Prior Harwin Securities. In the cases of Granville and Co. and Harvard Securities, if you take the trouble to search out their advertisements in the *Financial Times,* you will find a number of the shares, in which they make a market, listed together with the spread quoted by the dealer in the shares.

Licensed dealers (and Granville and Co., Harvard Securities and Prior Harwin Securities are only a few of the operators in this field) are governed by the Department of Trade under the Prevention of Fraud (Investments) Act, but no specific regulations apply to their over-the-counter activities. The Council for the Securities Industry, the City's principal self-regulatory watchdog, is only concerned that over-the-counter market makers abide by its rules for licensed dealers. However, the main dealers have been trying to launch an association to bring self regulation to the loosely governed market. These markets, like the Rule 163 markets, are high risk/high reward markets – the investor putting cash into shares of companies dealt in by the OTC markets, or by brokers and licensed dealers under Rule 163, must bear firmly in mind the Latin tag, *caveat emptor.*

In the case of the Rule 163 market this is essentially designed for occasional deals in the shares of football clubs, or other exotica. However a number of private companies have found it useful – due to the lack of reporting regulations – to create a market in their shares via Rule 163, using stockbrokers and licensed dealers. Hence the rationale of the Unlisted Securities Market – The Stock Exchange Council's strategy being to move such companies into the USM or leave them to go back to being completely private.

6

What to do about new issues

The Exco Issue – a case in point

Anybody who stagged the Exco International issue a few years ago, and was lucky enough to be allocated 50,000 shares, could have sold them for a handsome profit on the very first day's dealing. The shares streaked up to a premium of 46p, clearing a tidy £23,000 on a 50,000 share allocation.

Rothschild's, which handled the Exco flotation, only cashed cheques for £56,000 and over. Anything under that figure was returned to the unsuccessful stag with a letter saying he had had bad luck in the ballot; the cheque was only cashed if the stag won in the ballot and got his share allotment.

Since there was no downside risk (although the stags had no prior knowledge as to the level at which cheques would be cashed), and with a hefty capital gain within a week on the cards, not surprisingly the City's *cognoscenti* – institutional fund managers, stockbrokers and private investors – tried to get in on the Exco act. As a result, the issue was 62½ times oversubscribed. Believe it or not, that meant more cash being put up by a group of money brokers whose assets are their dealing wits, paired up with their telephones, than by the entire capitalisation of the largest clearing bank with all the latter's weight of prime sited high street branches and welter of highly profitable subsidiaries. Because of the massive oversubscription, Rothschild's was criticised for pitching the price too low. But the bank did so on the rationale of using a price/earnings multiple which lay between those of two other 'glamour' money broking groups, both of whose share prices had rocketed since they went public: Mercantile House Holdings (which owns the money brokers, Marshall's) and R. P. Martin, another money broking group.

Pitching the price right

Rothschild's was just following what had been (and still is) accepted wisdom culled from the early 1970s issue boom, when you couldn't open each Monday's *Financial Times* or *Daily Telegraph* without wading through pages and pages of four, five, or even six, 'offer for sale' prospectuses (set in the smallest type to include all the information called for by The Stock Exchange rules). A merchant bank would pitch the issue price of any of these issues – just as Rothschilds did with Exco – aiming to set the new issue share price at a level acceptable to the institutional investment managers. This strategy ensures that some 80 per cent of the shares being floated ends up in 'safe' hands.

This particular piece of merchant bank marketing strategy rests on the idea that, if all the shares in a public flotation ended up in the hands of the stags, the latter would promptly (and quite properly) sell them off on the first, or second, day of dealing, thus pushing the issue price of the shares to a discount. It can take a long time for a share which goes to a discount immediately after a flotation to recover, and the sponsoring merchant bank gets a bad reputation in the City as a new issue specialist and the City's fund managers have long memories.

Once that happens, the flow of new issue business going to that merchant bank slows down or disappears – and the bank misses out on the lucrative fees from underwriting an issue – not to mention the other sweeteners, which make new issue business so attractive to bankers, and so expensive for companies going public. The straight advertising costs (if the offer for sale goes in the *Financial Times* and the *Daily Telegraph*) are between £70,000 and £80,000, while the investigating accountant charges £100,000 to £150,000 so you can quickly see how the overall cost of going fully public ends up in the £250,000 to £550,000 range, or even £1 million in the case of the much publicised Amersham International flotation.

The dwindling flow of new issues

In fact, the total flow of new issues dwindled to a trickle between 1974 and 1980. This was partly because of the tax disadvantages of going fully public. Private companies have much more freedom of manoeuvre to reduce tax liability on capital gains and capital transfers – for example, by keeping a low dividend profile, and so keeping the value of their shares as low as possible when they come under the scrutiny of the Inland Revenue. Since the lean years, new issues have made a comeback and opportunities for stagging have grown. What is the explanation for the new issue comeback?

First, the private companies which are jumping on the Unlisted Securities Market bandwagon (see Chapter 5) do so on the tacit understanding that they can only 'rest' in the USM for a limited period of time. Once their profits get to a level which The Stock Exchange reckons justifies a fully public quotation, they are firmly urged to go for one.

The second reason has been the appearance of a number of glamour shares heavy on profits but light on assets which are coming on to the market, such as Exco, or the computer firms. The third reason is that the Government is spinning off chunks of the public sector to reduce its borrowing requirement, cases in point being Cable & Wireless (5½ times oversubscribed) and Amersham International.

Understanding the stagging arena

We started off by pointing out the profits which could have been made by stagging the Exco issue to the tune of 50,000 shares. What if you haven't got that sort of money? You don't have to have it so long as your cheques aren't cashed; you're only passing across a number of pieces of paper plus a number of application forms – of which more later.

The heavyweights in the City, that is the institutional fund managers, the stockbrokers, and the investment departments of merchant banks, don't worry about sending in small amounts of, say, £50,000. However, even a small firm of stockbrokers will be stagging to the tune of several million pounds, and they do face a downside risk because all the big cheques are cashed. Since the cash has to be borrowed from the banks, the superstags carry an interest cost for a few days, and the merchant bank sponsoring the issue cashes the big cheques to get the use of that money free for those few days by putting it out on the inter-bank market.

The big-time stags, such as the stockbrokers, have to get a fat enough premium on a new issue, by means of the profit, as the shares are marked up on first day's dealings to cover their interest costs. They try to calculate the probable extent of oversubscription, so that by using probability mathematics (or plain guesswork) they can try to judge how heavily scaled-down an allotment they will receive. The million-pound punters are always scaled down; it wouldn't have looked at all good if small investors were seen to have been frozen out of a new issue by sheer weight of mighty money. Oversubscribed issues go to a ballot, and the results of a typical ballot are shown in Fig. 5.

The pink letters

There's a mistaken concept about preferential allotment letters (usually pink). In theory these letters go to long-serving employees, managers and directors of the firm going public, so that they can participate from benefits of going fully public (the directors and senior executives will almost invariably have share stakes, anyway). In practice there's a brisk trade in preferential allotment letters, and only a very dim stockbroker fails to get hold of a line of allotment letters for his firm. The shrewd stockbroker sees that he gets his firm's share of allotment letters.

Improving your chances

The main problem is how to improve your chances of getting shares in an issue which is going to be heftily oversubscribed. Back in 1973, some issues were 100 times oversubscribed; one offering just happened to hit the market the day after Lord Wilberforce settled the miners' strike and was 142 times oversubscribed.

You have to watch the run-up to the new issue very closely indeed to get a view on just how many times it is likely to be oversubscribed. A follower of Exco's successful issue would probably have predicted that the issue was going to be oversubscribed between 50 and 100 times, judging by the views of the market experts, as relayed to the financial press, and that a certain amount of astute massaging by clever public relations would be done. With a pretty hefty oversubscription in prospect, the punter has to decide how high a premium he thinks the share will reach on the first day's dealing. In the case of Exco, the size of the premium *before the issue* was forecast at anything between 35p and £1 (it turned out to be 46p).

Some people are willing to accept the high risks involved of writing numerous cheques which they can't possibly cover and of trying to estimate at what rate the issuing house is going to cash them. It is a reasonable bet, if an issue is forecast to be oversubscribed 50 times or more, that the sponsor-

The Ballot for Associated British Ports

The Government floated off a £22 million offer in the form of a half share in Associated British Ports and received applications for shares worth almost £740 million by way of 156,000 applications for a total of 600 million shares. After rejecting suspected multiple applications, the lead underwriters, merchant bankers Schroder Wagg and Kleinwort Benson, dealt with the applications as follows:

Applications for 100 to 2,500 shares—weighted ballot for 100 shares, in multiples of 10 shares.

Applications for 3,000 to 9,500 shares—3.3 per cent of the amount applied for subject to a minimum of 100 shares, in multiples of 10 shares.

Applications for 10,000 to 24,000 shares—3 per cent of the amount applied for subject to a minimum of 100 shares, in multiples of 10 shares.

Applications for 25,000 to 90,000 shares—2.9 per cent of the amount applied for in multiples of 25 shares.

Applications for 100,000 shares and above—2.8 per cent of the amount applied for in multiples of 100 shares, subject to a maximum of 125,000 shares.

Fig. 5 The results of a typical ballot.

ing merchant bank won't bother to cash 'the small stuff' which may well mean anything under £20,000. (This does not apply to new USM issues as all cheques are liable to be cashed.) Therefore people can send in many cheques for, say £10,000 apiece, hoping that they won't all be cashed. To make any money from new issue stagging you have to deal in these sort of amounts because each successful application will be scaled down, as you can see from the example of Associated British Ports (Fig. 5).

The big advantages are that there should be no downside risk, the pay-off can be large and these people are a million times more likely to win than if they filled in pools coupons. However, this practice is not to be recommended.

7

What to do about rights issues

Many a perplexed shareholder in a company making a rights issue must wonder what to do about his or her 'rights' – whether to take up the rights, sell the rights in the market 'nil paid', sell enough rights to pay for the call on the shareholders' remaining entitlement, or whether to do nothing at all. Before going on to discuss these options, we will first examine why a company has a rights issue at all, whether it is in the best interests of the shareholders, and the consequent effects on the company's share price.

Why have a rights issue?

Essentially companies make rights issues to shareholders in order to raise finance with which to underpin an investment programme (money for new plant or to finance an aquisition) or to reduce the burden of company debt. Alternatively a company could be hard-pressed for cash and have to ask its shareholders to put up more cash because the necessary finance cannot be raised elsewhere. This latter case could be termed an 'involuntary' rights issue because the company has no alternative method open to it of raising the ready cash. The former case is basically a 'voluntary' rights issue because the company has the other options open to it of raising the necessary cash by selling equity to the investing public, or by arranging a term loan.

The flood of rights issues which took place in 1975, 1976 and 1983 was due mainly to the dire straits of the capital-raising market over the preceding periods and caused many companies to get an unbalanced share capital/debt ratio, with fixed debt taking too heavy a proportion of the company's capital base.

What about the shareholder?

Rights issues tend to be disliked by shareholders and by the City investment managers of insurance funds, of investment and unit trusts and of banks. A rights issue can (and most probably will) dilute the shareholder's return from the company in which he has invested because the rise in net profit on the new capital raised will usually be less than the increase in shareholders' capital.

It is first necessary to clear up a popular misconception which has probably been caused by the cosmetic effect of the name 'rights issue'. There are still many investors who believe that a rights issue by the company in which they hold shares offers them the opportunity of subscribing capital on preferential terms – in other words the shareholder is getting something for nothing. What is not fully understood, or perhaps not understood at all, is that the apparent discount between the price of new shares being issued by way of rights, as against the price of the old shares, is eliminated when the shares go 'ex-rights'. (The 'cum-rights' price is the market price of the shares before the rights issue.)

The rights will have a value only if the market believes that the new capital being raised will earn a rate of return the same as, or greater than, the existing share capital. In order to evaluate a rights issue it is necessary for the shareholder to know to what use the capital being raised by his company's rights issue is to be put, and what sort of return will be earned from it. This would enable him (if he believes the company's projections on future earnings per share) to make a decision as to whether he should do one of the following:

1 Subscribe new money.
2 Sell his rights 'nil paid'.
3 Do nothing.
4 Sell both his existing shareholding and his rights.

The common sense approach to a rights issue – remember that it is rare that rights issue capital will earn the same rate of return as the shareholders' existing capital in a company, particularly if the new money is only being used to fund existing debt – is to look at the actual arithmetic involved in working out the value of a 'right'.

Calculating the value of a right

In calculating the value of a right to a shareholder we have to make the unlikely assumption that the rights issue capital will earn the same rate of return when employed in the shareholder's company as does the existing capital.

In a rights issue, the new shares are always issued to the existing shareholders for a price lower than the prevailing market price at the time of the issue. The formula for calculating the value of one right is to take the difference between the ex-rights price and the subscription price, and divide it by the number of rights necessary to acquire one new share. The arithmetic is shown in a worked example (Table 5).

Table 5 The formula for calculating the value of a right

	No. of shares	Price per share	Total value
Existing shareholding	10	£2.00	£20.00
New shares	10	£1.00	£10.00
Total	20	£3.00	£30.00

£30 divided by 20 = £1.50, which is the ex-rights price.
The value of one right is calculated as follows:

Ex-rights price	£1.50
Subscription price	£1.00
Apparent gain	0.50p

Let us suppose that the Widget Manufacturing Company's shares have a prevailing market price of £2 per share. Widget makes a rights issue of ten new shares for every ten existing shares at £1 per share. The cum-rights price of a Widget's ordinary share is £2, the prevailing market price before the rights issue is made. The ex-rights price will be £1.50.

Rights issues are usually disliked by shareholders because their usual effect is to cause the company's share price to fall, owing to the 'dilution' effect. However, if the market is short of stock, a rights issue can offer the big institutional buyer the opportunity of translating surplus cash into equity, and the share price can rise. Normally, though, rights issues are more in the interests of the company than in its shareholders, and the shareholder has to be very certain about the future earnings potential of his company before taking up his rights to subscribe for new shares.

Rights issues – other options

The shareholder can, of course, sell his rights on the stock market on a 'nil paid' basis but keep his existing shareholding which has entitled him to those rights in the first place. All that 'nil paid' means is that the shareholder pays out nothing on the rights issue but tells his stockbroker to sell the rights on the market for what they will fetch. However, such a shareholder should be aware that in a despondent market any bonus effect (i.e. getting something for laying out nothing) from a rights issue can speedily be eliminated if the value of 'nil rights' is halved during a day's trading on the stock market. Selling your rights 'nil paid' depends on market conditions at the time of sale – and there is the broker's commission to come off what you might get for your 'nil paid' rights in the market place.

Another option open to the shareholder is to sell enough of his rights in the market to pay for the call on the remaining entitlement. There is rather a complex formula which calculates how many rights should be sold by the shareholder in order to render his subscription self-financing. This avenue is really only worth pursuing if you have a large shareholding.

If the shareholder chooses to do nothing at all, then either the company's other shareholders buy his entitlement by means of an excess application form, or the shares are sold in the market and the premium, if any, is distributed to the shareholder.

The last option of all and (depending on the individual company involved) perhaps the wisest, is for the shareholder to sell his existing holding along with his rights, collect any premium, and then reinvest the proceeds in another company giving a better chance of capital appreciation. This avoids the dilution effect of the rights issue. There is usually an exception to every rule, and in the case of rights issues the exception is provided by companies which use rights issues to get round dividend limitations.

8

The options market – a way of hedging your bets

If you turn to the 'Market Report' page of any day's *Financial Times* – assuming you're a *Financial Times* reader – you will find a small section headed 'Options'. Typically, the text will read as follows: 'Money was given for Hollis Bros., London and Liverpool, Polly Peck. . .' and another 20 or 30 company names will follow, depending on just how busy the options market has been on the previous day.

Later in the report you will read: 'Inter-City were dealt in for the put, while double options were arranged in BICC, North Kalgurlie, Rediffusion and Westminster Properties'. This is a typical daily list of options taken by investors on companies which, on that particular day, were the focus of speculative investment attention. The list of company names changes daily as investment interest moves on to other companies listed on The Stock Exchange – or the same names can crop up over and over again as speculators buzz, like bees around a honeypot, over a particular share which has the rumoured promise of prospective large, short-term, capital gains.

The main point to realise about the options market is that many a seasoned investor never uses it at all. It may seem to be a rather esoteric corner of the stock market, with incomprehensible jargon of its own, which is clearly only of interest to the professional operators inside the Square Mile of the City. In fact, the options market offers private investors very useful hedging opportunities against share prices falling or rising, and equally useful opportunities to 'gear up'. The latter piece of jargon simply means that a small outlay can be used to take up a position over a much larger number of shares than would be the case if the investor was buying the shares direct. Lastly, there is a little known opportunity open to wealthy private investors with large investment portfolios known as 'taking option money'.

The 'option' explained

The use of options is restricted to shares. You cannot take out an option on gilt-edged stocks. Options in gilts were once allowed – many years ago – but the use of gilt-edged options as a tax avoidance technique brought the Treasury down on the practice like a ton of bricks. You can take options over overseas shares (at extra cost) but it is worth remembering that during the era of exchange controls (1939–79) while, in theory, you could take out an option on an overseas share, in practice, the options market in such shares was virtually extinguished by the existence of the investment currency premium which had to be paid when buying overseas shares, or options thereon. If exchange control was to return, the investment currency premium would re-emerge and the market in options over overseas shares would shrivel as a result. Bear in mind that the Exchange Control Act 1947 (which formalised the controls which were imposed on the outbreak of war with Germany in 1939) was only suspended in 1979. The Act is still on the statute books so no new enabling legislation is required to restore exchange controls. In theory, at least, such controls could be re-imposed over, say, a week-end.

An 'option' is just what the name implies. Instead of buying a number of shares direct, the options market exists so that the investor can buy a three-month option over the same number of shares, but for a much smaller outlay. This is where the gearing effect comes in because a wealthy investor, by using the options market, releases capital which would be tied up in a direct share purchase for other more lucrative investment opportunities in shares, gilts or gold or he pursues the conservative strategy of leaving the bulk of his cash sitting on the wholesale money markets, earning a rate of interest. He has therefore no downside risk (other than the erosive effects of inflation) to worry about.

A worked example

Perhaps the best way of showing how an options contract works is by way of a worked example. Let's say you want to buy 5,000 shares in The Widget Manufacturing Company and the shares stand at £1. Instead of paying over £5,000 to buy 5,000 shares you have the alternative of buying an option over the same 5,000 shares for around 10 per cent of their market value. As you will see, you only lay out £500 instead of the full £5,000. (For purposes of simplicity, dealing costs for both the share purchase and the options purchase have been ignored.)

The gearing now comes into its own. If you had decided to buy the 5,000 shares direct it would have cost you £5,000, and if the shares had doubled within three months, the £5,000 would have risen to £10,000, so your capital gain is a handsome £5,000 (or 100 per cent).

Instead of spending that £5,000 you elect to take the options route and pay £500 to buy an option over the same number of shares. The 5,000 shares double in price to £10,000. The cost of exercising your option, at the option striking price of £1 per share (the market price prevailing at the time you took out your option), is £5,000. If you then sell your shares in the market, after they have doubled in value in that three months, you make a capital gain of £5,000. From this gain you have to deduct the cost of your option contract of £500 – but this still leaves you with a windfall profit of £4,500. To get this windfall you have only had to risk £500, so you have a 900 per cent return on that risk money. This is the gearing effect.

Of course, every silver lining has a cloud attached to it. The disadvantage of the options investment strategy is that, if the shares on which you buy an option go down in price, and the option isn't worth exercising, then you lose all your option money and you have a dead loss on your hands. Your £500 investment has been lost as surely as if you had backed a horse to win at Goodwood and that horse had failed to come in with even a place. However, since April 1978, you can trade options on certain shares (mainly high quality blue-chip shares) listed on The Stock Exchange before the options contract lapses – so you can get out before the date when the contract lapses and you don't have to take a dead loss.

The trouble with the traded options market (discussed in detail later in chapter 9) is that the number of companies in which options on shares can be traded is quite small – the market has never taken off in the way that its promoters thought it would. The initial reason for the lack of enthusiasm was to be found in the ridiculous tax treatment of traded options where a loss could be treated as a profit. This was put right a few years ago and traded options came under the capital gains tax rules, but the market still remains relatively feeble on the investment scene.

The traditional options market is much stronger and has been around for a long time. The actual mechanics of the market-place are simple enough, as you can see from Fig. 6 – a section of a timetable from a typical *Financial Times* option market report.

OPTIONS

First Deal-ings	Last Deal-ings	Last Declara-tion	For Settle-ment
Jan 24	Feb 4	May 3	May 16
Feb 7	Feb 18	May 19	May 31
Feb 28	Mar 11	June 2	June 13

Fig. 6 An extract from a *Financial Times* options market timetable (courtesy of the *Financial Times*).

You buy options contracts through your broker who then gets on to one of the options dealers who perform the jobbing function. As each new Stock Exchange account day opens, the option period is three months – a period which dwindles to 2½ months until the arrival of the next account day restores the option period to three months. As an option holder you are deemed to have abandoned your option unless it is exercised on the last declaration date (which you can see in Fig. 6) – a date which is shown on the contract note and which is normally 12 days before a Stock Exchange account day.

A *call option* is the commonest type of option, giving the owner the right to buy a number of shares three months ahead of that day's share price. In fact you do have to pay slightly over the odds because you pay a few pence more than the shares' current market price because you have to pay for the option broker's work which consists of making sure he can deliver those shares to you three months hence.

Put options are the opposite of call options, giving the right to sell a number of shares in three months' time at the market price prevailing for the shares at the time you take out your put option. It is an extension of the bear share operation principle – selling shares you don't have as you predict that the price will fall and that you will be able to buy back the shares at the lower price and make your profits that way. You can also use the put option technique for insurance purposes – for a modest outlay you can ensure the sale of your shareholdings at a known price in three months' time. This is the sort of insurance you could purchase three months before a General Election, for example, on a 'just in case' basis.

There is also a *double option*. This means you can exercise either a call option or a put option (but not both) three months ahead. As you might expect, a double option costs nearly double the price of a call or put option. Using double options is a technique to pursue if the share price is very volatile. The price has to rise or fall by a sizeable amount just to enable you to break even on the option money you have laid out. It's a technique which is useful in the gold share market – where alarming rises can quickly be accompanied by equally dramatic falls as gold bugs back their hunches on the future course of the gold price by buying and selling gold and gold shares.

Another little known facility which exists is 'taking option money'. Let's suppose you have £30,000 worth of shares in your portfolio. You can tell your broker that you are willing to sell an option on any or all of them. Your broker then advises an options dealer that your portfolio is on the market – and if he hears of an opportunity he will get in touch with your broker who then tells you what the terms of the offer are. Let's assume you have shares worth £3 apiece and you tell your broker you would like option money of 30p a share with an option exercise price of £3.03. If the shares go up in price, the option is exercised and you sell your shares for £3.03 per share plus the 30p option money (but less the option dealer's cut and your broker's commission). If the price of your share falls and the option is not exercised then you keep your shares but you get the option money (less expenses) of 30p per share for your pains.

9

Trading in options

There is an interesting little corner of the stock market which should appeal to those who take what you might call a lively speculative interest in shares (meaning the realistic approach, which is that the stock market is better designed for the gambler than for raising finance for British industry). That corner is *traded options*. In the *Financial Times*, you'll see a list of traded options on the page dealing with The London Stock Exchange. Don't be put off because it looks complicated at first sight. Once you know what you're letting yourself in for, and you are armed with the information you need to play the traded options market, it is possible to make big gains from taking the right positions.

Initially, profits from traded options were treated by the Inland Revenue as 'wasting assets' for tax purposes, so that an apparent profit on traded options could be transformed into a loss. The profits from traded options are now covered under the normal capital gains tax rules.

The big bonus provided by the traded options market is that you are not locked in to your original decision as in the case of the traditional options market dealt with earlier. You can buy and sell a traded option through the stock market at any time before its maturity, taking your profit when you wish (just as you can with a share purchase) and still come out with some of your capital if the speculation turns sour and you have to sell at a loss.

Options – a brief recap

The long-established market in options dealt with earlier (pages 32–35) is something different. To recap, an option is a device which allows you, instead of buying a number of shares directly, to purchase a three-month option to buy the same shares, for a much smaller outlay than the normal purchase costs. You use a call option if you reckon the shares will go up; a put option is what you buy if you think they'll go down; while a double option lets you make an 'each-way' bet in a wildly gyrating stock market.

The options market is a way of putting a limited amount of money to maximum use, but the trouble with it is lack of flexibility. It is a case of heads you win; tails you lose the lot. Either the investor exercises his option on maturity, or lets it lapse – hence the dead loss on his gamble if the share price doesn't move in his favour.

Options trading doesn't have this defect. It was introduced in April 1978 in London, following the lead of The Netherlands which launched traded options (the European Options Exchange) in Amsterdam. There is still only a handful of blue-chip company shares – BP, Grand Met, Shell and the like – in which you can trade options.

The mechanics of the market-place

Just like the traditional London call option, the premium paid for a traded option is only a percentage of the prevailing market price of the underlying share. That's why and how the speculator can buy an interest in many more shares by using options than by buying the related share outright. The market men talk about 'gearing' or 'leverage' – both of which mean getting much more action from a limited amount of capital.

The jargon of the market-place

Class of options: All call options relating to the same underlying share form a single class.
Series of options: All options of the same class which have the same exercise price and expiry date and which relate to the same number of shares form a single series.
Expiry dates: When trading in an option is established you have a choice of three expiry dates – three, six and nine months ahead.

Land Securities traded options (to take one example) are described in detail in Table 6.

Table 6 Land Securities traded options

Share price	Exercise price	Price of traded options		
		(July)	(October)	(January)
325p	323p	13p	29p	26p
	353p	2p	13p	9p

The choice of three expiry dates gives you July, October and January, hence Land Securities July Series, October Series and January Series. At each expiry date the 'exercise prices' are either 323p and 353p (i.e. that's what the option entitles you to buy the underlying shares for). So there is Land Securities 323p and Land Securities 353p. When the July option expires, a new nine-month series, finishing in April, will be opened for trading.

Price or premium

The price (or premium) of the option in each series fluctuates according to supply and demand in the market. This is governed by the following three things:

1 The price of the underlying share.
2 The striking price of the option.
3 The length of its life.

The two exercise prices of Land Securities are 323p and 353p, and the shares stand at 325p in the stock market. The price for July 323p shares is 13p and for July 353p shares it is 2p. As you can readily appreciate, while the Land Securities share price stands at 325p in the market, the July 323p shares are worth 2p (325p − 323p = 2p) against the traded option price of 13p. However the July 353p shares are without intrinsic value because the exercise price is greater than the share price (353p, as against 325p).

The reason why the traded options prices increase, with the July 323p shares at 13p, against the January price of 26p, is because an option with a life of six to nine months is obviously more valuable than one with a life of only three months. I say 'obviously' because there is a greater opportunity for the underlying share to grow in value over the longer period.

'In the money . . . out of the money'

An option with an exercise price below that of the underlying share price is said to be 'in the money'. If the exercise price is higher than the share price, the option, conversely, is 'out of the money'. The number of shares to which a single option contract relates is normally 1,000. If you want to trade in the options on 5,000 shares, you place an order for five contracts, *not* for 5,000 options.

An example

What does this mean for the speculator? Suppose that the shares of A. Company Ltd stand at 400p. There are three series of traded options – the July 380s, which are at a 40p premium, the July 410s, which are at 15p, and the July 440s, which are at 5p.

Leaving aside dealing expenses for the moment, the speculator could buy 500 shares for £2,000 or alternatively two July 380 contracts for £800, plus five July 410 contracts for £750, plus 10 July 440 contracts at 5p (or 10 contracts) for £500. If he buys the shares direct, then he gains or loses as the share price moves, and he remains the owner of the shares until he decides to sell them. However, just look at the speculator's position as against the movement in the underlying share price shown in Table 7.

Table 7 Share price at expiry date of options

Outright purchase	Cost £	380p £	400p £	420p £	440p £	460p £	480p £
500 shares @ 400p	2,000	−100	Break even	+100	+200	+300	+400
or							
Two July 380 contracts @ 40p	800	−800	−400	Break even	+400	+800	+1,200
Five July 410 contracts @ 15p	750	−750	−750	−250	+750	+1,750	+2,750
Ten July 440 contracts @ 5p	500	−500	−500	−500	−500	+1,500	+3,500

The rewards can be high

Looking at the figures you catch the point of both traded options and gearing, and with it some of the excitement of successful speculation. The outright buyer of 500 shares at £4 apiece makes only a £400 profit if the share price moves up by 80p. The man who gambles longest – for nine months – and bets on the share price rising furthest by buying £500 worth of July 440 contracts (10 of them) at 5p makes £3,500 once the share price reaches 480p. The outright buyer has had to lay out £2,000 to make £400. The high risk speculator has laid out £500 to make £3,500.

Remember, though, the point of this market – that you don't have to wait three, six or nine months to cash in. The profits can be taken through the market whenever you feel like it – the next day after purchase if you get really lucky, because the market price of the traded option will fluctuate with the price of the underlying share.

One of the more radical changes in the traded options market came in 1983 when overseas specialist dealers were given direct access to the London stock market to trade on their own account as dealers. The market was opened to traded options experts whether they come from Chicago, any other overseas market, or the UK. The one caveat is that they have to be accredited to one of the jobbing firms already transacting business on the floor.

10

Convertibles – the two-way investment

'Convertibles' are not popular among the investing public as an alternative to investing in ordinary shares directly or in unit or investment trusts, gilt-edged stock or to placing money on deposit with banks, local authorities or with building societies. The main reason is that many private investors are not sure just what sort of animal a convertible stock is and how they should evaluate it.

A convertible is an investment which occupies a sector somewhere between fixed-interest stocks and equities. By buying a convertible, the investor gets a fixed annual income which is determined by the market price he has paid for the convertible, and by its 'nominal' rate of interest. For example, a buyer of convertible stock with an interest rate of 9½ per cent for each £100 nominal worth of stock, who pays a market price of £70 for the latter, can work out his annual income as follows:

$$\frac{9\tfrac{1}{2}\% \times \text{£}100 \text{ nominal}}{\text{£}70 \text{ market price}} = 13.57\% \text{ (a yield of £13.57 for every £100 invested).}$$

In addition, the investor gains a further option which is not available to the buyer of the 'straight' fixed-interest stock. He buys the opportunity to convert his loan stock into the particular company's ordinary shares at a known price during a predetermined future period. It is essential to bear in mind from the outset that the movements in the market price of a convertible loan stock closely follow the price of the company's shares.

There are a number of varieties of convertible loan stocks which are quoted on The Stock Exchange. The bulk of convertibles bought and sold are of the 'straight' variety. These account for around four-fifths of the market in terms of nominal (as opposed to market) value. Next in order of importance are the 'partly convertible' loan stocks which account for about one-tenth of the market. These give the buyer the right to convert part of his investment into the ordinary shares of the company at some future date. 'Subscription' stocks give the buyer an income plus the right to subscribe cash for shares in a company at a future date. 'Warrants' provide the buyer with no income, but do provide the right to subscribe cash for shares at a future date – and are of obvious interest to high tax payers. Then there are the sterling/dollar (and sterling/other 'hard' currencies) convertibles which provide a fixed income payable in sterling, plus the option to convert into United States or other overseas equities at a future date.

The advantages of convertibles to the investor

By buying a convertible, the investor is buying an insurance 'cushion'. If the investor buys shares in a company, the price of the shares can be subject to very volatile movements. A convertible does not fall so far (in terms of the market price) in a bear market as does the price of the related share. The other side of the picture, of course, is that the price of a convertible does not move up as high as the price of the ordinary share during a bull market. But the 'cushion' effect of convertibles comes into its own in a really vicious bear market (such as 1974) when the market price of the convertible reaches a 'floor' when its yield becomes equal to that of fixed-interest securities which have no conversion rights.

Another advantage of convertibles is that the income they provide is normally higher than that provided by way of dividend from the company's ordinary shares, and there is the additional sweetener that this income is safer than ordinary share dividends. In fact, both income and capital invested in, and arising from, convertible loan stocks are safer than ordinary shares because, in the event of a liquidation, convertibles are repaid before shares. This being said, it is worth uttering a word of caution. Convertibles are normally issued by companies on an unsecured basis for the very good reason that this relieves the company from reducing the amount of chargeable assets available for further borrowing. Therefore, if a company 'goes to the wall', although the convertible stock holder gets preferential treatment (which is not given to the ordinary shareholder) he is still part and parcel of the unsecured creditors so far as the liquidator is concerned.

What other advantages are there for the investor in convertibles? In addition to the guaranteed capital appreciation (as long as the stock is bought for less than its nominal value) before the exercise of the conversion rights, there are potential rewards accruing from participation, even after the conversion rights are exercised, in a growth-oriented company. In the long term, cool analysis may provide the answer that the risk to the private investor in buying convertible loan stocks, issued by growth-oriented companies, may be less than the risk of erosion of his capital by inflation if he is keeping it on deposit over the same period. In fact, when the clouds of economic gloom settle menacingly on the investment horizon, the convertible, particularly the short-dated convertible standing at below its nominal value, becomes an attractive 'hedge' investment.

Who issues convertibles and why

To the company issuing the convertibles, the stock provides a better opportunity to raise capital – possibly to be used to finance an acquisition, for which the rate of interest will be lower – than that for straight (non-convertible) loan. This device also avoids the necessity of watering down the company's own equity base, which would happen if more ordinary shares were issued. The effect of the future conversion rights on the convertible loan stock is to create deferred ordinary shares at a higher price level than the prevailing market price at the time of issue, whereas ordinary shares issues are normally made at a discount to the prevailing market price.

Who issues convertibles? Most stem from the financial sector – banks, property companies (which account for around one-fifth of the convertibles issued) and investment trusts. During the bear market of 1974–75 a number of companies and investment trusts were to the forefront in 'buying back' their own convertible loan stocks. For example, investment trusts can reduce the prospective dilution in their own shares (after the conversion rights are exercised) by buying back their convertible loan stock. A cash-rich manufacturing company can also avoid this dilution by buying back when it believes that its convertible loan stock is oversold owing to adverse market sentiment, and that the yield it provides has reached an abnormal level.

Other points of interest about convertibles are that well over half of all convertibles issued are for amounts of under £5 million, but account for only one-fifth of the market. Nearly 20 per cent of convertibles are for amounts of over £10 million, but account for well over half the market in terms of nominal value.

The premium

The biggest pitfall for the investor when he wants to buy convertible loan stock is how to evaluate the 'premium' which will tell him whether the convertible in question is 'cheap' or 'dear'.

The premium is the difference between the market price of a company's ordinary shares and the effective conversion price of the related convertible loan stock. The premium is the price you pay for the extra safety provided by the convertible. As a general yardstick, in normal market conditions, if the premium is more than three times the difference between the convertible's yield and the yield offered by the related ordinary share, then the convertible is a 'dear' buy'.

How do you work out the premium? In order to explain this I will now give a worked example. (Bear in mind at the outset that the extra cost, or premium of an investment in a convertible loan stock, is expressed as a percentage of the cost of the equity in the convertible loan stock.)

Let us suppose that the price of a convertible loan stock in the Widget Company is £56 per £100 nominal during a time of high inflation and high interest rates. The conversion terms are 200 shares in the Widget Company for every £100 nominal of stock held, giving a nominal conversion price of 50p as against, let's say, the market price of 15p per Widget ordinary share. This means that the investor buying the loan stock at £56 buys conversion rights into 200 shares – an effective market price of 28p.

The premium for the conversion rights is 28p less 15p (the effective conversion price of the convertible loan stock less the current market price of Widget's shares) which is 13p. The difference of 13p compared with the market price of 15p throws up a premium of 13/15 or 86.7 per cent – a very high premium so the Widget convertible is a dear buy even though it is offering a running yield of 16.7 per cent. The premium can, of course, be small, or negative (at a discount).

11

Warrants – a gambler's market

In the Square Mile of the City of London, the pundits will tell you that warrants are for experts only, and that the spectacular increases and precipitous falls in warrant prices, allied with the lack of understanding as to just what the warrant market is all about, render investment in warrants a hazardous business for the amateur. There certainly is some truth in the argument that warrants experience price fluctuations which are much more volatile than ordinary shares. For example, if you had had the good fortune to buy shares in January 1975 then you would have been unlucky if you had not doubled your money within three months by investing in any representative selection of blue-chip shares. However, had you invested in, say, Cavenham warrants at the same time, your capital would have produced more than a 500 per cent increase over the same period. There is certainly a lack of understanding about the warrants market, and the experts swathe their manipulations with all the mystical mumbo jumbo of 'gearing effects', 'conversion premiums' and 'volatility factors', which can cause the amateur to retreat in dismay.

What are warrants?

Warrants present only capital gain opportunities and do not pay the holder any income. Therein lies their secret. High tax payers, for obvious reasons, are not interested in income but they are interested in capital gain because the latter attracts a much lower rate of tax. Warrants, which really had their heyday back in the bull market of 1972, are pieces of paper, issued by a company or by an investment trust, which give the buyer an option to buy a predetermined number of the company's ordinary shares at a predetermined price during a predetermined period of time in the future.

In theory at least the warrant provides three additional benefits to the buyer. One is that, instead of locking up money in a slab of a company's ordinary shares, the investor can buy warrants giving him rights to buy the same number of shares at a known price sometime in the future for, normally, a fraction of the cost. This means that he releases his capital to pursue other investment opportunities. Let us take for our example a share, perhaps in an investment trust, which has a market price of 51p. A holding of 10,000 shares would cost the shareholder (exclusive of the dealing expenses) £5,100. However, the investor has the alternative of buying the same investment trust's warrants for 19p which gives him the right to convert them into the same shares, on the basis of one share per warrant, at a price of £1 until, say, the year 1990. This means that rights over the same 10,000 shares will 'only' cost him £1,900, thus releasing £3,200 for investment elsewhere. And in the heyday of speculation, when punters borrow cash with which to finance their stock market operations, the warrant technique maximises their capital gain opportunities.

A second benefit provided by warrants is that of liquidity. Buying warrants does not mean that you have to lock up cash for several years. The existence of an active market in which you can buy and sell warrants means that you can turn them into cash if need be.

A third benefit is that, along with the fact that warrants can produce much greater capital gains opportunities when the stock market is recovering from a really vicious bear market, the price of warrants does not fall as far as the price of the related ordinary shares when shareholders panic to sell during a bear market. The reason for this is that the warrant price, being normally a fraction of the price of the related ordinary share, sooner or later falls to a point beyond which it can fall no further. It joins the ranks of the 'penny stocks', and even though the price of the ordinary share still has some way to fall, the price of the warrant cannot become a negative amount so long as the company which has issued it stays solvent. So when the market turns, the warrants can chalk up really spectacular gains in the initial buying rush as the professionals scent the opportunity to make a massive capital gain by buying warrants, giving them rights to shares at a set price.

The 'gearing effect'

The opportunities for big capital gains are provided (and here we come to our first bit of jargon) by the 'gearing effect'. The price of warrants moves in the same direction as the price of the shares to which they are linked. However, in percentage terms, the price of warrants moves up faster in a bull market, and goes down faster in a bear market, before stopping at the 'penny stock' floor. To take a practical example of the gearing effect at work, suppose a share worth £1 in the market has related warrants entitling the holder to buy shares in the company at £1 at the end of five years, and these warrants are quoted in the market at 35p. If the ordinary share price rises to

£1.10 (an increase of 10 per cent), the effect of this rise could be to push up the value of the warrants to 40p (an increase of 14.3 per cent). Thus the warrant price would have gone up faster than the share price, but the same would be true in a downward movement; the fall would be correspondingly steeper.

Why do warrants exist?

Investment trusts have been prolific issuers of warrants principally for technical reasons. Back in the heady bull market days of 1972 investment trusts had something of a marketing problem. In an investment trust 'offer for sale' it was difficult to persuade investors to buy shares in the investment trust at the offer price – 'at par' – because investment trust shares then (and now, too) stood at a hefty discount to their net asset value. Warrants were therefore issued to overcome this problem, and were offered as a particular sweetener to the high tax-paying investor. Many of the warrants available on today's stock market are left over from the early 1970s. In the company sector, the companies involved are either in property or in former high flying shares which fell from grace.

Warrants – tips to remember

The main point to bear in mind about warrants is that the price at which a warrant is bought and sold on the stock market is entirely separate from the subscription price, which is the predetermined price at which the warrant can be converted into a company's ordinary shares at a predetermined date in the future.

Going back to our example of the hypothetical investment trust warrant, this entitles the holder to one share on the final exercise date, which is in 1990, at a subscription price of £1 per share. The investment trust warrant can be bought and sold in today's market for 19p. The investment trust ordinary share can be bought and sold in today's market for 51p.

The 'conversion premium' which the experts talk about is simply the premium you pay for buying warrants against buying the same company's ordinary shares. I have worked out an example to show you how to work out the conversion premium. Let us suppose a company has shares currently quoted at 40p per 10p ordinary share. The warrants issued by the company are quoted at 12p. The warrants give the holder the right to subscribe for one share in the company (cost £1.35) at any time between 1989 and 1993. The arithmetic for working out the conversion premium is as follows:

Warrant market price	12p
Warrant conversion price	135p
	147p
Less: market value of company's ordinary share	40p
	107p

The conversion premium = $\frac{107p}{40p}$ = 267 per cent

As you can readily see from the example, the conversion premium is the theoretical extra price (over and above the cost of the company's ordinary shares) which the investor pays when he buys a warrant at its quoted price – assuming he will hold it to maturity and then exercise his conversion rights (at 135 pence per share in the example).

The 'volatility factor' bandied about by the warrant market experts just means price fluctuations under another pseudo-scientific name. It is supposed to provide some indication of how speculative the warrants are in the light of the frequency of the price movements (volatility) of the underlying share to which the warrant is linked. The more volatile the share price, the more attractive are the warrants, because they present the holder with more frequent opportunities to buy and sell, and so increase the rate of his capital gains opportunities (or, it should be stressed, the rate of his capital losses).

The best way to evaluate warrants is not to attach too much importance to gearing ratios and volatility factors but to use your common sense and always bear in mind that warrants are a gambler's market. Warrants, like racehorses, fundamentally have a set of odds attached to them. The high risk-reward ratio could be assessed just as well by a bookmaker as by a warrant expert at 16-7 against or 5-4 on, if he took the trouble to discover just what ingredients make up 'the form'.

The three golden rules to remember are as follows:

1 The warrant market is a gambler's market.
2 Ask yourself if the warrant you are buying gives you a good deal in commonsensical terms.
3 Work out the likely effect on the warrant price of the movement in the underlying share price.

12

The unit trust world – 'good in parts'

The background

There are 569 unit trusts available to UK investors. The number of unit holders investing directly in unit trusts is around the 1.9 million mark, while 2.6 million UK residents invest indirectly in unit trusts via unit-linked insurance policies. The value of funds managed by the unit trust 'industry' is £9,721 million at the time of writing. Each month a proportion of the units held by unit holders is cashed in. Annual repurchases, as a percentage of total funds invested by Britain's unit trusts, have varied during the last decade between 4 per cent and 9 per cent.

Why do unit trusts exist at all, given the number of trusts on the market and the large number of people who use them? They were first formed – and this still provides their main rationale for existence – to offer the individual investor a chance to spread his risk by buying units in a unit trust. The 'unit' is invested in a balanced portfolio of shares. In theory this technique of 'pooling' a large number of small investors into one buying organisation – a unit trust – is marketed to the general investing public as being a better method of investment in ordinary shares for the smaller investor than if he goes it alone, does his own selection and buys his own shares in just a few share sectors. Additionally, the unit trust buyer gets rid of the headaches (and some of the fun) of running his own investment portfolio by handing over the job and attendant paper work to the unit trust company's professional management. The assets of the funds are held by independent trustees so security is reasonably assured.

Types of unit trusts

The marketing experts at the unit trusts have thought up all sorts of gimmicks over the years to attract the investing public, and they have had a fruitful background against which to work – as private investors have increasingly pulled out of the stock market and as stockbrokers and investment managers have swung towards catering for the big customers like the pension funds and the insurance companies. By being so aggressive, the unit trust industry has partly cooked its own goose. Unit trusts have been formed, and advertised with large-budget advertising programmes for every conceivable purpose, and there are now far too many of them.

Trusts have been formed to cater for those who want high income, for those who want capital gains, for those who want a combination of both, for North Sea oil, for motorway construction, for investment in firms involved in commodities trading, for investment in various stock markets overseas, and for gold investment (or rather investment in gold mining companies). You name it, the unit trust industry has probably thought about it.

Management charges

'What,' you ask, 'do the unit trust management companies get out of it?' In this country, unit trust management companies make a charge of around 5 per cent initially (some charge 3¼ per cent) which is known in the trade as 'front-end loading'. Part of this front-end loading is available as a kickback – or, more cosmetically, 'introductory commission' – to insurance brokers, stockbrokers and recognised agents who bring business to the unit trust. In addition there is an annual management charge of ¾ or 1 per cent when the initial fee is 5 per cent, which is based on the value of the funds under management. These figures may not sound very much, but what it boils down to is that if you invest £10,000 in a unit trust, as a result of the front-end loading, the value of your capital is reduced immediately to £9,500. This is all very well if the value of your capital is increased by astute investment management by more than the front-end loading and annual management charge, but relatively few unit trusts manage to beat even the *Financial Times* 30 share index. Hence the reason why the great British investing public has become increasingly disenchanted with unit trusts as a form of investment.

Bid and offer prices

The 'bid' price is the price at which the unit trust management will buy back units. The 'offer' price is the price at which the managers will sell the units. The spread between bid and offer prices varies between unit trusts – generally it is around 7 per cent which incorporates the initial fee. The bid price of the units is decided by the market value of the unit trust's shares, cash and accumulated income. The offer price is related to the market value of the unit trust's assets plus expenses.

Units in unit trusts can be bought and sold at any time. In fact unit trusts are allowed only to invest in quoted Stock Exchange securities.

Methods of investing in unit trusts

There are a variety of ways in which you can invest in unit trusts. You can either put in a lump sum, save as you earn with monthly savings plans, or you can link regular savings plans to life insurance (with certain tax advantages). You can also exchange your existing, directly purchased shares for units. The share exchange scheme works as follows. If you have 1,000 shares whose market bid price is 100p and whose offer price is 105p, you could sell them through a broker for £1,000, less commission, contract stamp and VAT (£16.50), and make £983.50. However, if the shares happen to be shares which the unit trust company is prepared to add to its own portfolio (usually UK or overseas blue-chips) then it will buy them from you at either half the difference between the bid price and the offer price (102½p) or at the full offer price (105p) and credit you with units to that value. But if the unit trust company does not wish to add your shares to its portfolio, it will normally sell them for you and then pass on to you the full bid value in units. Bear in mind that an exchange of shares for units in a unit trust is regarded as a disposal for capital gains tax purposes.

The tax position

At this point it is worth talking a little more about the tax position on unit trusts. So far as income tax is concerned, with each distribution of income from a unit trust, the unit holder gets a voucher detailing the income and the tax credit relating to it, which together make up the income for tax purposes. The tax credit is equivalent to tax at the basic rate of tax, and no further tax is due from unit holders attracting tax at the basic rate. Unit holders with an excess of personal reliefs to set against their unit trust income can reclaim all or part of the tax credit from the Inland Revenue. Conversely, unit holders liable to tax at a higher rate or to the investment income surcharge will have additional tax to pay.

As for capital gains tax, a holding in a unit trust is a chargeable asset for CGT purposes and you have to show purchases and sales on your tax return form. Losses arising on the disposal of units can be offset against other gains made in the same year. Any balance remaining can be carried forward and set against gains in later years. The extra tax relief mentioned earlier in connection with unit-trust-linked insurance schemes arises from the fact that such schemes are a variation of an ordinary life insurance arrangement except that the premiums are invested in unit trusts. A major attraction is that you can get tax relief on the premiums.

Unit trust selection

The performance of unit trusts is good only in parts. When we said at the outset that investors, by buying units in a unit trust, were ridding themselves of the worry of making their own investment decisions, this was only partially true. The prospective unit trust buyer is still left with two crucial investment decisions. One is when to buy units in a unit trust. If he gets in at the bottom of the stock market and gets out at the top, he can still increase his capital even within the confines of an average performance unit trust. Bear in mind, though, that unit trusts remain fully invested in shares at all times, whether in the UK or overseas. So when a really vicious bear market develops, as in 1974, the unit holder is carried down inexorably as share prices slide. If he remains a private (direct) investor, and gets his timing right, then he always has the opportunity of turning his shares into cash. However, because of the front-end loading involved in unit trust buying – they are really long-term investments – it takes a long time for the unit trust to make up, in performance terms, the 5 per cent you lose at the outset.

The lesson of history is that the average member of the investing public has tended to buy units in unit trusts when the stock market is nearing the peak of a bull market, and then starts to unload (sometimes in panic) when the market is near the bottom. This 'herd instinct' buying pattern by unit trust customers has resulted in the professionals regarding an upsurge in unit trust buying as signalling the peak of a bull market – and time to get out. Such behaviour also enables the professionals to unload part of their holdings at the top end of a bull market to the unit trusts, providing them with a convenient outlet but without disturbing the market too much.

The other point to bear in mind is that having long-term investments is a mug's game, whether it be in shares, gilts, commodities or unit trusts. Unless you are very lucky indeed, you cannot buy units in a unit trust (or even in a unit trust whose purpose in life is to buy units in other unit trusts) and then sit back and watch your capital increase steadily year by year. One year's star unit trust may be next year's dud, so you are still left with the problem of moving in and out of unit trusts operating in diverse fields in the UK and overseas. And the front-end loading factor each time you buy means that you are trying to pursue a successful investment policy with one arm tied behind your back.

Looking at performance tables (e.g. Table 8) and selecting the unit trust which tops the table can lose you your money. In fact you could make out quite a good argument for picking out the bottom performing unit trust in one year as a good investment for the next. Perhaps a more reliable guide might be provided by sustained performance over a period of years.

Table 8 1983 unit trust performances

How £1,000 invested on 1 November 1982 would have grown or fallen if sold on 1 November 1983, including reinvested income.

The best unit trusts (by type)	£
Fidelity Japan	2,013
Crescent Tokyo	1,928
Abbey Japan	1,888
GT European	1,927
Henderson Europe	1,854
Barrington Europe	1,745
Oppenheimer International	1,659
Henderson International	1,519
Arbuthnot Foreign	1,465
Prolific Technology	1,608
Brown Shipley Technology	1,530
S & P New Technology	1,487
Oppenheimer Special Situations	1,542
Schroder Smaller Companies	1,486
Fidelity Special Situations	1,485
Aitken Hume Energy	1,525
Target Commodity	1,421
Tyndall Natural Resources	1,369
GT US & General	1,507
M & G American Recovery	1,496
Target US Special Bond	1,486

The worst unit trusts	£
Britannia Preference	840
HK Extra Income	907
Chieftain Preference	916
HK Commodity	920
Arbuthnot Gilt	935
Arbuthnot Preference	933
HK Income	938
Key Fixed Interest	941
Schroder Gilt	945
Cater Allen Gilt	949

(Source: *Money Management.*)

13

Investment trusts – the sleeping giants

Investment trusts have been around for a long time on the investment scene. They go back over a century or more to when investment trusts were first formed to channel money into projects requiring large amounts of investment capital – for example, the railway networks in the USA. Throughout the twentieth century they steadily expanded and, by 1972, they had reached the £7 billion mark when measured against the value of the assets under their management. A decade later the assets under the management of the UK's investment trust community had swollen to over £11.5 billion invested in 214 trusts owned by 250,000 shareholders.

Investment trusts – the background

For much of the period since the last war, investment trusts were regarded as sleeping giants. Cross shareholdings within trusts protected the trusts' managers against unwelcome invasions and thereby provided job security to the trusts' managers and directors. After all, you can't really blame them – the investment trusts are companies, and any company's management tends to like job security and will go to some lengths to ensure it.

For many years, in the 1950s and 1960s, the investment trust concept was unfamiliar to the UK investing public, as against the better known (but much more recent) unit trusts. There are good reasons why this unfamiliarity has persisted. One major difference between unit trusts and investment trusts is that the latter are not allowed to advertise their wares, whereas most potential investors are familiar with the unit trust advertisements in the Sunday editions of newspapers, or the billboard advertisements at the wealthier commuter stations around London.

The reason for the investment trusts' inability to advertise is that no company is allowed to advertise its own shares for sale. An investment trust, being a company, is in the same boat as any other company. To give chapter and verse, an investor in an investment trust buys shares in a limited liability company, and the latter is subject to the dictates of the Companies Acts 1948 and 1967 which prohibit the advertisement of a company's own shares for sale (apart from the occasions when a company joins the unlisted securities market or goes fully public via a full Stock Exchange quotation).

By contrast, an investor who buys units in a unit trust buys them in a trust fund authorised by the Department of Trade. The unit trust managers can advertise their wares at any time, and the fact that there is a strong life insurance link with the unit trust movement means that savings schemes keyed to the unit trust movement via the insurance link has led to fairly aggressive hard selling techniques. Hard selling because the life insurance salesmen can sell such schemes on a door-to-door basis – collecting, for their pains, a generous cut by way of introductory commission from the front-end loading which is part and parcel of all unit trusts.

In fact, the only time an investment trust company can advertise its attractions to the investing public is when it is first launched; after that initial launching, only its annual results can be advertised.

Another major difference between an investment trust company and a unit trust is that an investment trust company, like any other limited liability company, has a fixed amount of capital and hence comes the term that an investment trust is a 'close-ended fund'. The point of the latter is that the capital of the trust need not be increased if the conditions on the investment scene are unfavourable – for example, during a bear market when it would be foolish for the managers to go on buying up lines of shares, when the share prices are dropping continually. Unit trusts, on the other hand, are 'open ended' and the managers of the unit trust can make available more units or buy back existing units, whenever required by the unit holders. The 'open-ended' effect does tend to give unit trust managers a feeling that they should fully invest in shares at all times – whether in a bull or bear market. However, given the fact that most unit trust groups invest in overseas markets in addition to that of the UK, they can invest in a counter cyclical fashion to the UK 'bull' and 'bear' cycles by buying shares in markets overseas which are going up – when the UK market is set on a downward path.

Investment trusts do have one significant advantage over unit trusts – the freedom they enjoy in investing in a wide range of assets including unlisted companies and property. Unit trusts are generally limited to quoted companies.

There are other differences between investment trusts and unit trusts. For example, units in unit trusts are normally bought from, and sold back to, the managers of the trust – with a 'spread' of some 5 per cent between the 'bid' and 'offer' price of the units, giving rise to the term 'front-end loading'. By contrast, shares in investment trusts – as is the case with shares in any other quoted company – are bought and sold via the stock market at the ruling market price when the bargain is struck between stockbroker and jobber.

Another difference between investment trusts and unit trusts is that investment trusts, like any other company, can borrow money or 'gear up'. Unit trusts can only issue equity units, which means that they cannot borrow more money than the unit holders have made available to the unit trusts' managers. Yet another difference is that investment trusts can hold back part of their profits (accruing from dividends and capital gain) for further investment, while, on the whole, unit trusts distribute their income. It is worth noting, however, that some unit trusts do provide re-investment facilities via 'accumulator units'.

In the old days of exchange controls, which lasted for 40 years from 1939 (they were imposed on the outbreak of war) to October 1979, investment trusts did have an advantage over unit trusts. Investment trust companies could borrow in foreign currencies to buy overseas shares – thus avoiding paying the investment currency 'premium' which at one point was over the 50 per cent mark. Unit trusts could only raise 'reciprocal' or 'back to back' loans for overseas investment. These involved making an equivalent amount of sterling available in the UK to the overseas lender. While exchange controls have been suspended since October 1979, the Exchange Control Act 1947 remains on the statute book. Should controls be re-imposed, the investment trusts would win back their overseas investment advantage.

The 'discount' factor

Shares in investment trust companies are dealt with on The Stock Exchange in the same way as any other publicly quoted share, hence the price of the shares depends on supply and demand in the market place. The big difference between investment trust shares and other publicly quoted shares lies in 'the discount factor'. This is the discount between the worth of the investment trusts' underlying portfolio of shares and the market capitalisation of the investment trust concerned (the price of the trust's shares multiplied by the number of shares on the market). A more technical description would involve the valuation of a trust's investments and its current assets, the deduction of the current liabilities plus prior charges (such as fixed-interest loans) and the comparison of that value with its market capitalisation. An investment trust company's shares are described as being 'at a discount' when the market price of the shares is less than the net asset value of the shares. They are 'at a premium' when the reverse holds true.

The trouble is, of course, that investment trust shares – with a few exceptions from time to time such as the Japanese-oriented UK investment trusts – have been 'at a discount' throughout the 1970s and 1980s. Back in

1972 when investment trusts had a popular year – a situation resulting in 40 new investment trusts being created to capitalise on the situation (and resulting in an oversupply of investment trust shares which was to hang heavily over this particular market-place for many a year) – the discount was only 5 per cent. In the gloomy years of 1974, when the *Financial Times* 30 share index slumped to under 150, the discount on investment trusts rose to approaching 40 per cent. By 1983 the discount had narrowed a little — to around the 26 per cent mark – but was still massively higher than the level last seen in 1972.

Varieties of investment trusts

There are a number of varieties of investment trusts catering for the tastes of just about every type of investor – whether seeking to invest in a particular part of the world, such as the Far East, or the United States, whether seeking to invest in a particular industrial sector, or seeking income or capital gain only.

The 'orthodox' investment trust is the one with the longest established history, and the orthodox trusts constitute the bulk of the 190 members of the Investment Trust Association. There are some investment trusts – private companies – which aren't members of the Association, but the latter encompasses 95 per cent of the market if measured in terms of the assets under their control.

The orthodox trust is the investment trust which uses straight equity, or ordinary share capital, with which to invest, supported with loan capital sometimes. The trusts use the capital at the managers' disposal to invest in UK or overseas shares or both. In fact, the main attraction of investment trusts is that they give UK investors – particularly the private investors who would find dealing with an overseas stock market difficult (in Japan, for example, the investor can only deal in 1,000 share lots) – access to overseas shares. They can thus avoid a bear market in the UK by investing in an overseas market with growth potential. Investment trusts provide one way to protect an investment portfolio against the cyclical down turns of the UK stock market.

'Split-level' trusts

Most of the refinements of the investment trust world have been the products of the past two decades. 'Split-level' investment trusts were introduced as one refinement back in the mid-1960s. The technical jargon is 'split-capital' trusts and the idea behind them was, and is, to give the prospective shareholder a choice of capital gain, income, or a combination of both. Examples of split-level investment trusts are 'Dualvest', or 'Triplevest'. The share capital of such trusts is divided into two sections – 'income' shares and 'capital' shares. Some also offer debenture and preference shares. The investor who wants income, buys income shares, while the high taxpayer can elect to buy the capital shares, thus getting capital gain which is taxed at a far lower rate than unearned income.

Unlike the orthodox investment trust company, the split-level trusts normally have a fixed life during which all, or most of, the income is paid out to the income shareholders. When the investment trust company is finally liquidated at the end of the day, the income shares are repaid at a pre-arranged price and the remaining assets of the liquidated trusts go to the capital shareholders. The latter route is of obvious interest to those who wish to go without income in favour of capital appreciation in the future.

Other types

There are also the 'B' shares investment trusts. 'B' shareholders have equal rights with the ordinary shareholders in investment trusts but they normally have no rights to dividends. Instead, each 'B' shareholder receives a scrip issue, with an asset value equal to the amount of the dividend paid on each ordinary share, which can be converted into ordinary shares at a future date. Again, this route is of interest to high tax payers because scrip issues are not taxable as income they are attractive to investors seeking capital growth.

An investor in investment trusts also has the option of buying debenture and loan stocks issued by investment trust companies. This particular strategy is of interest to the low taxpayer who seeks income rather than capital gain. The stocks have conversion dates fixed to become effective sometime in the future and have specified rights to be converted into the investment trust's ordinary shares at a price around the trust's asset value at the date of first issue. This route is of interest to those seeking income – with the potential capital gain arising in the fullness of time when the stock is converted into ordinary shares. This is a 'belt and braces approach' for those who want the best of both worlds – income now and capital gain later.

Last, but not least, are the warrants. These are transferable certificates, which can be bought and sold on the stock market, which give the holder the right to subscribe for shares in an investment trust at a future date. This route is for the speculator who is only interested in capital gain because warrants give the investor 'leverage' or 'gearing up' opportunities and they give the buyer an option on a future interest in the ordinary shares of an investment trust for a small initial investment. Warrants carry no dividend entitlement or capital gains tax liability until the warrant holder exercises the option into ordinary shares. The warrant route, which can be used with ordinary shares generally, not just with investment trust shares, is a strategy to use if the investor doesn't want income, but seeks capital gain in the future. The 'leverage' facility means the investor can take a large prospective position over investment trust ordinary shares for a relatively small outlay.

The sleeping giants

With all these different options open to the investor – particularly the small investor who can spread his risks by buying shares in an investment trust, in just the same way that he can spread his risks by buying units in a unit trust (but without paying any front-end loading) – it is surprising that the investment trusts haven't become more popular. Indeed, for much of the last decade, investment trusts were labelled 'the sleeping giants'. This image clouded their attractions despite the fact that they offer the private investor the opportunity of handing over his cash to a highly trained professional manager. There are only The Stock Exchange dealing costs to pay on share purchase and sale – amounting to some 5½ per cent. There are investment trusts catering for every need, whether for those investors seeking diversification outside the United Kingdom on the share front, for investors seeking to invest in a particular industrial sector (such as North Sea oil), for investors seeking capital gain, for investors seeking income, or for investors seeking a combination of the two.

An attractive enough situation, yet for much of the last 15 years, the investment trusts have not been attractive either to the private investor or to the institutional investor seeking to diversify his portfolio outside the United Kingdom since exchange controls were removed in 1979. Since then the institutional investment manager has been free to invest directly in overseas markets, rather than by way of an investment trust, and has not had problems about paying the investment currency premium or arranging 'back to back' loans. The lack of interest, the oversupply of investment trust shares as a result of the 1972 creation of 40 new trusts, and the competitive attractions of unit trusts produced a malaise around investment trust shares. This malaise produced the hefty discount between the market price of investment trust shares and the worth of their underlying investments. In the late 1970s the investment managers of the trusts were trying to find a way to shake off the 'sleeping giant' image.

They had a difficult problem on their hands and much of this problem lay in their own complacent attitude over the past years. The British investing public had become steadily less interested in investment trusts as they, and their professional advisers (some very hard selling professional advisers, at that – particularly the insurance broking fraternity) had been attracted to unit trusts and investment bonds. The big investment trust shareholders, such as the insurance companies, had begun to lose interest, mainly because they could invest overseas directly. Overall, less money was going into the ordinary share market anyway, and consequently there was an even greater loss of interest in investment trusts.

There were several options open to the investment trust managers. One option was to mop up the oversupply of shares on the market by buying their own shares back – and the necessary legislation to enable them to do so was passed in the Finance Act 1982. It must be stressed that the 'share buy back' legislation was not passed to help the investment trust industry but was passed as a down-to-earth measure to assist the private company sector (in which many a minority shareholder was enmeshed without the possibility of having his shares bought out by the company in which he, or his forebears, had invested).

Another option was 'unitisation'. In other words, the investment trusts could transform themselves into a more readily marketable unit trust. There was (and still is) a good deal of misgiving about this particular course of action. Many investment trust managers believe that the 'unitisation' route would lead to a heavy outflow by their big institutional shareholders once they received units in exchange for the investment trust shares. The investment managers of the investment trusts didn't (and still don't) want to start a rush for the door by using the unitisation technique.

With some trepidation some investment trusts have decided to take the 'unitisation' route. Early in 1983, Touche Remnant, one of Britain's largest managers of institutional investments, unveiled its plans for breaking into the unit trust market and promoting its image among small investors by launching three specialist and one general unit trust with assets worth £50 million. The specialist fields of three of the four trusts were carved out of a defunct investment trust – Cedar Investment Trust. The specialist fields were overseas investment, income growth and special opportunities. The shareholders in the Cedar Investment Trust, whose demise had been announced in the previous March, opted to convert 51 per cent of their holdings into the new, general, unit trust. Of the remaining shareholdings, 24 per cent were put into the overseas unit trust specialising in the United States and the Far East, 19 per cent went into the income growth trust and 6 per cent into the special opportunities trust.

This was a classic carve up of an investment trust into four unit trusts – with the Touche Remnant people anticipating that at least half of the previous shareholding in Cedar (mainly the holdings owned by the institutions) would be cashed in over the six months following the 'unitisation' announcement. The reason behind the move was to escape from the stringent advertising restrictions on investment trusts and Touche earmarked a six-figure sum for a three-week advertising campaign to boost the new unit trusts.

Another example of unitisation was provided by Schroder Wagg's Broadstone, with £54 million worth of assets, and two small American, specialist trusts (run by Williams and Glyn's) also took the unitisation route.

In addition to the investment trust managers' ideas as to the boosting of their image, the whole industry got something of a shot in the arm in 1977 when the first flurry of takeover activity took place. This was due to the fact that institutional fund managers – especially the pension fund managers into whose coffers flowed ever greater streams of cash as the British worker became more pension conscious – woke up to the fact that they could buy large blocks of shares at less than their market price by buying up a whole investment trust whose market capitalisation stood at a substantial discount to the trust's underlying blocks of shares. The concept was that, had the same pension fund been engaged in buying the same shares through the stock market, the very weight of its buying muscle – quite apart from the fact that the pension fund would have been paying the full market price for the shares – would quickly drive up the price of the share against it. The takeover activity has continued apace. In 1983, for example, Throgmorton Trust, with assets of £83 million, launched an unfriendly bid of £52 million for Edinburgh's Pentland Investment Trust.

Strategy

The strategy of the investor and his posture to the investment trust sector has already been discussed in this chapter in parts. For example, the investor seeking capital gain will have a greater inclination to delve into the investment trust warrants on offer than the investor who seeks income.

The spate of bids, unitisations (or 'capital reorganisations' as they are more euphemistically called), new specialist funds and increasing efforts by the Association of Investment Trust Companies to persuade the private investor that they are a viable alternative to unit trusts was underpinned in the early 1980s by one other factor. By 1983 the average annual management charges of investment trusts stood at one third of 1 per cent – a considerable attraction, bearing in mind that unit trust management charges had been substantially increased in the previous year. The tax treatment of investment trusts still remained more favourable than the tax treatment of unit trusts.

Investment trusts – tax treatment

Investment trust companies do offer very real tax advantages. Corporation tax is effectively charged on the capital gains of an investment trust company at a concessionary rate equivalent to one half the basic rate of income tax. Double taxation of the investment trust company and its shareholders is prevented by giving the shareholder a tax credit at one half the basic rate of income tax on any gains he may realise on disposal. This credit reduces his own liability to capital gains tax and is available irrespective of the amount of gain which the investment trust company has itself realised. The effect of this tax sweetener is that no payment is required from a shareholder liable to tax on his capital gains at half the basic rate of income tax.

So far as income tax is concerned, the shareholder receives his dividend plus a statement of the income tax credit applicable to that dividend. The total amount of the dividend and the tax credit is set against any liability to tax on that income. A shareholder liable to income tax at the basic rate has no further tax to pay and if he is not liable to income tax he can claim repayment from the Inland Revenue.

Picking the trusts

While a positive way of looking at investment trusts is that a private investor can buy, say, £125 worth of assets for £100, the reverse side of the argument is that the same investor is going to get a capital gain only either if the discount narrows considerably, or if the trust is the subject of a bid, or (marginally) if the trust unitises itself. This applies to investment trusts generally – getting down to a specific example, one method of selecting investment trusts is to buy shares in those trusts which are well known. The rationale is that those which try hardest to cultivate their stock market image are likely to do best in future. Investment trusts which communicate with the big investing institutions, benefiting from their financial muscle, tend to see their shares perform better than trusts which lack the will to communicate.

Another option is to invest in one of the unit trusts which themselves specialise in investment trust shares. Their performance over the two years to the end of 1982 was monitored by Planned Savings and is shown in Table 9.

Table 9 Unit trusts which invest in investment trusts

	Percentage capital gain over the two years to the end of 1982
Abbey Investments	22.5
Britannia	19.4
James Finlay	29.2
Kleinwort Benson	24.8
M & G	21.1
Practical*	24.9
S & P	20.2
Target Investments	25.0

(Gains include reinvested income.)
(*Practical is a management company acquired by Oppenheimer Fund Managers.)

Yet another option is to pick a trust which is vulnerable to a predator – City analysts reckon that a spate of bids will halve the number of investment trusts over the next five years.

14

The gilt market – something for everyone

The lesson to be learned from the history of investment in gilt-edged stocks is that the long-term holder, who buys for income and then settles back to collect year in, year out, loses money. Long-term holders of Government stock who may have bought in the 1940s, 1950s and early 1960s will have seen a substantial proportion of their capital wiped out both in nominal terms – because the price of Government stock has sunk steadily as interest rates have risen – and also in real terms because of inflation. After a period of disillusionment, investors returned to the gilt market in substantial numbers in 1976 and 1977, lured by the attraction of high interest rates.

There is money to be made from gilts, whether you want income, capital gains or a combination of both, but only if you operate a proper gilt-edged investment policy. If you do not like the headaches which go with carrying out your own gilt investment policy, there are gilt-edged funds which will do the job for you.

Background

Gilt-edged stock is issued periodically by the UK Government when it needs funds. Stock is issued with a fixed or floating coupon or rate of interest, and the par value of the stock is paid at redemption (i.e. you collect £100 for every £100 nominal).

Until the mid-1950s, Government stock was the bulwark of the investment market. Respectable investors, whether private or corporate, relied mainly on gilts as the major investment sector open to them. Ordinary shares, even in a publicly-quoted company, were for the speculative investor. Consequently, companies had to pay a much higher rate of dividend than was provided by gilts because the latter could offer the investor complete security. Today the position is reversed, and yields on gilts can offer double the yield provided by ordinary shares. The other fact to remember is that for 20 years after the last war, the 'natural' rate of interest was thought of as 2½ per cent. When interest rates started creeping up to the 6 and 7 per cent mark there were howls of anguish, which may seem ludicrous to us now, with the Minimum Lending Rate having touched 17 per cent in the autumn of 1979. The 1960s and (particularly) the 1970s witnessed gilt yields being forced higher and higher (and prices dropping lower and lower) due to the twin stimuli of ever-increasing interest rates – allied to the Government need to raise money with which to finance public sector expenditure – and ever-increasing rates of inflation.

Why do investors buy gilts?

Firstly, there is the sweetener that if you hold gilts for longer than a year, there is no liability to capital gains tax, unlike equities. If you buy gilts which are on the National Savings Register (forms for this are available at Post Offices) income is paid gross before tax, but you can only buy £5,000 nominal of any one stock at any one time.

Secondly, interest rates can move down as well as up, so individuals and institutions, particularly insurance companies, need the essential factor of certainty for their calculations. By buying gilts giving a guaranteed yield of, say 11 per cent over a seven-year period, it is possible to match the maturity date with some other aspect of investment (perhaps the provision of an annuity) with complete certainty. Equally, an individual requiring the assurance of a guaranteed income for the rest of his life of, say, 14 per cent, could buy undated Government stock. Both the insurance company and the individual are protected against any further interest rate changes. If the interest rate structure moves down, then they still get their 11 per cent and 14 per cent respectively. If the interest rates move further up then they still have the same certainty, except that they have lost the opportunity of achieving an even higher yield. You cannot get this certainty from the volatile, short-term money markets.

The other reason for buying gilts is capital gain. If interest rates move down, the investor can sell his gilts for a capital gain (alternatively, if interest rates move further up then a capital loss is accrued). Both capital gains and capital losses are chargeable and offsettable against capital gains tax if gilts are bought and sold within a year.

The rewards of operating a shrewd gilt-edged switching policy can be very great if the investor gets his buying and selling decisions right. Bear in mind that the further away the date of the gilt-edged stock and the lower the coupon, the greater is the price movement in response to a change in the yield structure. Another change which took place in the structure of the gilt market at the beginning of the 1970s was a realisation of the importance of equivalent gross yields. The capital profit potential was indicated by low-coupon stocks and the discount between the market price and the gilt's nominal value. A specialised market in low-coupon stocks emerged with one very important factor in its favour. 'Tap' stock issues carried increasingly higher coupons. The low-coupon stocks still in issue today are a hangover from low-interest rate eras, and the amount in issue is steadily being reduced by redemptions.

Excluding undated stocks, the nominal amount of low-coupon stocks (below 5 per cent) in issue in 1971 was £5,104 million. By 1976 this had dropped to £3,362 million and by 1981 the total had fallen to £1,750 million. This represents a sector of the gilt-edged market where supply does not increase, but is steadily going down, while demand from taxpayers can – when the prospects look bright and interest rates look like moving down – be high. Low-coupon gilts are particularly attractive to investors in high tax brackets for the very good reason that all gilts are free of capital gains tax if held for over one year.

Longer-term gilts

In the case of longer-term gilt-edged stocks, the situation is rather different because stocks in this category are bought for their tax advantages and are affected by investors' expectations as to the future rate of inflation. Demand for high-coupon stocks is maintained to a substantial extent by the cash flow of the pension funds and insurance companies which are always potential buyers of these investments. While shorter-dated stocks cannot free themselves from the countervailing influences of money market rates, longer-dated gilts are influenced to a much greater extent by the expectations of the institutional investment managers who are prepared to look beyond short-run circumstances. In this sector the investor may be prepared to accept the risk of a long-dated security, despite the fact that the improvement in circumstances which has led him to buy may be several months away.

For those prepared to take the risk that interest rates will fall, the rewards are very high. At the time of writing 'real' interest rates at the undated end of the gilt market are about negative if we allow for inflation and tax. But, if long-term interest rates fell by 30 per cent over the next three years – from, say, 13 per cent to 8 per cent – gilt prices would rise by 45 per cent. If this took place, which would be very agreeable, the investor would find himself still in receipt of a 13 per cent income, plus the added bonus that the value of his capital would have risen by half as much again.

Political consideration

Perhaps this is the point at which to sound a word of political warning. The cost of funding the national debt by means of gilt issues is now astronomically high compared with the 7 per cent average the Government paid only a few years ago. The Government has to fund its debt regardless of cost, otherwise the country itself would go bankrupt. The money has to be found to pay social security benefits, the salaries of those working in the public sector, the Government's investment programme, etc. If the money was not there then the Government's position would be exactly the same as that of a bank which has run out of money and has to close its doors. So the Government must turn to a supranational bank for credit (the IMF) and also pay the institutional investment managers the rates of interest (15 per cent or more in the autumn of 1976) required if those managers are to continue to lend to HMG. The introduction of a floating-rate Government stock has been one way of lowering the cost of financing Government debt but floating-rate stocks are unattractive to pension funds and insurance companies (the biggest gilt buyers) because they like to work on the basis of fixed rates in order to get their future sums right.

Remember that if you buy your gilts – through the Post Office, your bank manager, accountant or solicitor – via the National Savings Register route then you collect your interest gross before tax. This appeals not only to the non-taxpayer but also the taxpayer who can put the interest to work until he has to pay his tax bill; it is known as the 'interest on interest' factor.

Gilt-edged funds

If you want to avoid the bother of continually buying and selling in the gilt-edged market, there are investment vehicles known as gilt-edged funds which will do the work for you in return for a management fee. Actually, to call them funds is something of a misnomer: they are, in effect, gilt-edged portfolio management services which give private individuals a chance to achieve the same results on the gilt markets as do the big investment institutions. The service involves pooling a large number of relatively small amounts of cash available for gilt-edged investment and treating them as one large fund. The advantages of this pooling arrangement are that the clients get access to investment management which is normally only available to the big institutional funds, and that the economies of scale – in terms of commissions paid and administration costs – can be passed on.

The charges to gain access to this gilt-edged management service are 1¼ per cent at the outset and then ½ per cent per annum, with a minimal annual fee of £40–£50. The size of the management fee means that you really need to have at least £5,000 to invest in the fund to make the operation worthwhile.

Every investor who joins the service retains a 'beneficial interest' in his investment and is in much the same position as if he had entrusted his gilt-edged investment portfolio to the fund as a private client. But the fund has full discretion in investment policy on the gilt market and each individual's portfolio is tailored to ensure that a uniform policy is pursued.

In order to provide an 'index of value' the overall gilt-edged portfolio (the master fund) is valued and divided to show the value on a scale based on

£100 invested (the first valuation throwing up the index base of 100). The index is then published fortnightly in the *Financial Times* so that each investor can establish easily the approximate value of his portfolio and see how well his fund managers are performing on the gilt market.

There is an 'income portfolio' for the basic taxpayer, and a 'capital portfolio' for the higher rate taxpayer who seeks capital gains rather than income for the obvious tax advantages. There is no minimum amount of money which can be invested in the funds, although the annual minimum management charge rules out the very small investor. A bank is the custodian of the funds, and income distributions are made twice a year. By the way, a tip worth remembering is that a commission of half the initial charge (less expenses) is usually paid to introductory agents, so it is worth your while to feed your cash through to a gilt-edged fund via your accountants in return for reduced accountancy fees to yourself.

15

Gilts for capital gain, index-linked gilts and variable-rate gilts

Gilts for capital gain

There is no doubt about the fact that those with capital are penalised. Penalised, that is, for prudence and financial foresight on their own behalf, or resulting from that of their forebears. The penalty is felt most by those who put aside savings during their working lives in order to have an investment portfolio which can bring in an income with which to supplement their pension. They are taxed in full on that 'unearned income' – ironically earned from accumulated capital which has already paid tax. There is no earned income relief. If the investment income is high enough, the 15 per cent investment income surcharge is imposed.

One answer for those with capital suffering a high tax rate is presented by the low coupon gilts available on the stock market – gilts specially designed for what was once known as 'the surtax payer'. The concept of the low coupon gilt is simple enough – the market price of the gilt stands at a substantial discount to the redemption price.

Once the gilt is bought, the buyer knows that if he holds the gilt to redemption, he will get a built-in, guaranteed, tax-free capital gain. For example, Transport 3 per cent 1978-88 can be bought for say, £81.25 at the time of writing. On redemption – and the Government can redeem the gilt at any time up to the end of 1988 – the buyer gets back £100 for every £88.25 invested, presenting him with a capital gain of £11.75. In addition he gets a small running income from this low coupon gilt of approaching 4 per cent annually. The best buys among the low coupon gilts are to be found in the medium-dated (5- to 15-year maturities) sector of the gilt market. (See Table 10 for examples of these.)

All the gilts listed in Table 10 – there are others in the 'short' (lives of up to five years) and 'long' (lives of over 15 years) sectors of the gilt market – can be bought via the National Savings Register, with the exception of Gas

Table 10 Low coupon medium-dated gilts

		Market price* (£)	Interest coupon (per cent)
Transport 3 per cent	1978–88	77.25	3.8
Treasury 5 per cent	1986–89	79.50	6.43
Funding 5¾ per cent	1987–91	76.50	7.74
Funding 6 per cent	1993	70.75	8.44
Gas 3 per cent	1990–95	54.25	5.63
Redemption 3 per cent	1986–96	52.25	5.88

*At the time of writing, gilt prices move daily, as does the interest coupon.

3 per cent 1990–95. The advantage of dealing via the National Savings Register via main post offices is that dealing costs are lower than buying via a stockbroker or bank. Dealing costs are 0.4 per cent – or £8 per £2,000 worth of gilts bought. Up to £5,000 worth of gilts can be bought in this way at any one time using form GSI (G) which is available, along with a pre-paid envelope, from main post offices. If you wish to sell gilts before they mature, use form GS3.

Stripping gilts is an investment strategy which sounds as if it should be done in private between consenting adults. The rationale for 'gilt stripping' or local authority 'yearling bonds' stripping is to convert highly-taxed income into nil-, or low-taxed, capital gain.

It is an alternative strategy to buying low coupon gilts, and is of interest to the high rate taxpayer, particularly if the investment income surcharge comes into play. The 'gilt stripper' normally operates within a five-month period. The technique of gilt stripping is to buy high coupon gilts and sell them 'full of interest' prior to the first interest payment date. This rolls up the interest payment, which would be subject to unearned income tax at the recipient's marginal tax rate, into capital gain as the gilt is sold in the stock market at a price which takes account of the interest entitlement. In the market the practice is described by the professionals as 'stripping' or as 'selling dirty'. And a number of gilt and bond 'laundries' have established themselves in the City to buy in gilts and bonds full of interest from investors and sell them on to tax exempt institutions such as pension funds.

To strip gilts the investor must keep a careful watch on his diary. Gilt strippers concentrate on the short end of the gilt market (lives of up to five years) because this sector is less vulnerable to price fluctuation (and therefore the risk of a capital loss) than the medium and long term gilts.

Between interest payments on gilts there is an average period of 146 days (the period can be 145 days or 148 days, depending on public holidays). A short gilt has one day when it is 'clean' – which is market parlance meaning there is no interest accruing to it – and this is the best date to buy. The gilt then starts accruing interest and for maximum benefit should be sold on day 146 – on the last day when it is quoted 'full of interest' to convert the full, accrued interest into capital gain. Once you have sold you may well receive an interest payment on a gilt, or on a local authority bond, and may be tempted to cash this until you are asked to repay. Don't succumb to this temptation as this will imperil the whole gilt-stripping operation – return the interest payment to your broker, uncashed.

So far as the Inland Revenue's stance is concerned this gilt (or bond) stripping is a grey area. The Inland Revenue can decide to attack the whole transaction and translate all the 'capital gain' as income and tax it as such – particularly if the gilt-stripping technique is carried out too frequently. And you can't sell a gilt 'full of interest' and then buy the same gilt back, cleaned, the day after, and repeat the process *ad infinitum*. This will bring you under the bond-washing rules devised some years ago and your gilt capital gain will be treated as income and taxed as such. You should also bear in mind that, even at the short end of the market, prices can fluctuate for all sorts of reasons, presenting you with a capital loss on the gilt price front which may wipe out the rolled up income 'gain'.

Index-linked gilts

A relatively new phenomenon on the gilt market is the index-linked gilt. These are the gilts which guarantee that, for every £100 nominal worth of the gilt you buy, you will be repaid, on maturity, with £100 plus the increment thrown up by the increase in the retail price index. In other words, by buying such gilts, you are protecting yourself against inflation – you will get the real value of your capital back on maturity. And, to sweeten the investment, there is also a small yearly rate of interest over and above the index-linked provisions.

The Government broker has plans to increase the number of index-linked gilts on offer (see Table 11) until they offer a reasonably comprehensive cover across a maturity spectrum covering, say, 25 years. This does present the private investor who is willing to lock up cash – for a low current return – for a number of years with a guaranteed hedge against the erosive effects of inflation.

Table 11 The index-linked gilts on offer

Treasury 2 per cent	1988
Treasury 2 per cent	1990
Treasury 2 per cent	1996
Treasury 2½ per cent	2001
Treasury 2½ per cent	2003
Treasury 2 per cent	2006
Treasury 2½ per cent	2009
Treasury 2½ per cent	2011
Treasury 2½ per cent	2016
Treasury 2½ per cent	2020

Variable rate gilts

One way to protect yourself against losses on fixed coupon gilt dealings is to use the avenue provided by the variable rate gilts. Each variable rate gilt pays interest half-yearly at an annual rate one half per cent above the daily average of the discount rate on 91 day Treasury Bills over the previous six-month period. The object of variable rate gilts is to protect your capital against the risks of fluctuations as interest rates change. The effective rate of interest paid on the gilt automatically adjusts to market trends without any change in capital value.

16

What there is for you in single premium bonds

Investment bonds are often called single premium bonds. Over the past ten years the investment bond market has mushroomed. There are two reasons for this growth. One is the investment attraction of the bond for the investor. The second is the attraction that running bond schemes holds for insurance companies which stand behind the market, many with linked unit trusts.

These are the attractions

First, the attractions for the investor. Bonds can be a useful investment medium for three- to five-year periods during which you can build up cash – perhaps for retirement, or for payment of school fees, or to pay off your mortgage, or just because you want to make your cash grow.

The cash you hand over in the form of a single premium is managed for you, and the investment bond market has split itself up to cater for all varieties of investment taste – whether you seek what is absolutely safe and secure, or look for greater risk, coupled with the chance of greater capital appreciation.

Bonds are a tax-efficient form of investment. That's one of the reasons why they have drawn so much cash away from unit trust investment and straight stock market investment. The essential principle behind bonds is that you exchange your marginal rate of tax for the privileged tax 'shelter' of an insurance company. In addition, bonds linked to life insurance schemes attract tax relief on the insurance premium element.

The higher-rate taxpayer can take out 5 per cent of his capital free of all tax each year for up to 20 years – and, if he wants to take out more, this first 'free slice' lowers his marginal rate of tax on second and subsequent slices. And so, for the chap in his 50s who knows he is going to retire in say, five years' time and is already on a high rate of tax, whether on earned or unearned income, the bond facility gives him the opportunity of phasing his bond encashment so that it falls due when his tax rate drops on his retirement. This is really a method of deferring and reducing tax in that, if you are paying tax at the top marginal rate of 75 per cent and you know that you will be dropping back to, say, 40 per cent on retirement, it makes sense to defer your tax liability until the lower threshold is reached.

If you are looking for capital gain there is no personal liability to capital gains tax on encashment of a bond so this is a method of increasing your capital if the bond you select from the hundreds on offer happens to perform well. Furthermore, there is the virtue of liquidity. You can buy, or sell, bonds at any time through the management company operating the bond facility. At least one property bond, though, has a caveat that the managers can defer payment on a bond for six months. However, this caveat has not been invoked so far.

The above are the 'bull' points about single premium investment bonds. It is worth clearing up one matter before moving on to the 'bear factors'. There is a belief that investment bonds are free of capital gains tax. This is true, as we have just pointed out, once the bond encashment is in the hands of the investor. The reason is that the bond management company has already paid out CGT before encashment. Admittedly this is at a lower rate – around 20 per cent against the CGT rate of 30 per cent – owing to the use of offsets by the bond management company. However, when you bear in mind that the first slice of your capital gain in a year is exempt from CGT (after off-setting losses and taking into account indexation) the fact that CGT is paid by the bond management company is a disadvantage. This, therefore, is one of the snags.

Now for the 'bear' points. The first to remember is that, as in all investment markets, the institution or person selling a bond scheme – be it an insurance company, a unit trust or a stockbroker – makes money from it. Insurance companies with links with bond management companies, or indeed, independent bond management companies, make their money in two main ways. One is from the front-end loading. In the vast majority of cases the front-end loading, which is the percentage difference between the 'bid' and 'offered' prices, is over 5 per cent. The bid price is the price at which the managers will buy your bonds and the offered price is the price at which you buy the bonds from them.

Since in nearly every case the front-end load is slightly over 5 per cent, this means that, if you invest £10,000, you lose £500 initially. That £500 has to be made up by the bond investment managers before you get back to break even on your original capital. In some cases the front-end loading is over 8 per cent.

In a few cases only a bid price is given. Where no bid and offer price is quoted, you can usually assume that the management charges will be higher by way of compensation to the managers of the fund. The normal annual management charge for bonds quoted with a 5 per cent spread between bid and offer prices is ½ per cent.

Not that all the 5 per cent front-end loading goes to the bond-management company. Of this 5 per cent, 3½ per cent is available by way of introductory commission to those bringing bond business to the company – insurance brokers, bankers, solicitors and accountants. The size of the commission is one of the reasons that insurance brokers aim to include investment bonds in a client's overall investment strategy. After all, if a bond holder is investing £100,000, a kickback of £3,500 is a welcome source of income. And even on a £10,000 bond the introductory commission of £350 is well worth having.

Now let's explain the various types of bonds structured to meet your particular investment profile – whether you are averse to risk or are reasonably speculative.

The types of bonds

Equity bonds are self-explanatory. The bonds exist for investment in ordinary shares in the United Kingdom or overseas. While equity bonds are the highest-risk bonds, they have also brought the highest rewards.

The next category is *property bonds*. They invest in industrial and commercial property. The *managed bonds* spread risk by being in different sectors of the market place – equities, fixed interest, money, property – and being there at the right time. In theory the best managed bond should comfortably outpace the best of the equity bonds, but this hasn't happened in practice.

Fixed-interest bonds offer greater security than equity bonds, in theory at least, because they invest in Government gilt-edged stock and fixed-interest company stock. So they know, pretty well, what their yield is and they can give guaranteed rates of return.

Money bonds act as 'funk-holes' when the equity market, the gilt market and the property market become unsteady. When they totter it makes sense for the bond manager to go liquid (convert his shares into cash) if he can – which is doubtful in the case of a property-oriented bond.

The money bond invests its surplus cash in ultra-secure homes on the wholesale money markets (the interbank market or the local authority market) and in short-term money market 'instruments' such as Treasury Bills and Sterling Certificates of Deposit. When the other markets, e.g. the stock market, start rising, the cash is switched out of the money bond and into the equity bond – or it would be, if perfect investment managers were at work.

When money is pooled

What about the mechanics of the investment bonds? They are simple enough. Private investors pool their money in the bond of their choice and the bond issues units to bond holders in proportion to the money they have invested. The units can be bought and sold at any time from, and to, the bond management company.

Normally the minimum investment is £500, but you can go into some bonds with as little as £50, while other bond managers, who don't want the small fry, insist on a £2,000 minimum. There are no dealing costs. You can buy the bonds through a newspaper advertisement or through your bank manager, accountant or solicitor.

The professionals – principally insurance brokers who are great users of bonds in their tax-planning schemes – collect the commission from the bond management company. Essentially though it comes out of your pocket, not the pocket of the company, as the 3½ per cent introductory commission itself comes out of the 5 per cent front-end loading.

In the case of newspaper advertisements, the bond management company saves the introductory commission but has to pay for the cost of the advertising space, again from the front-end loading.

You are protected to a large extent by the stringent financial standards to which a bond company has to conform in order to gain the necessary authorisation to carry on bond-issuing business from the Department of Trade. And, in the dire event of a life assurance company failing, bond-holders would be covered by the Policyholders Protection Act under which policyholders get back at least 90 per cent of what they owned when the company failed. (By the way, the insurance element of a bond is usually quite small, so you should not assume that the holding of a single premium bond also meets your total insurance needs.)

Switching between bonds

You can switch from one bond to another within the same group. For example, if you feel that the time is ripe to switch out of an equity bond – because you think the stock market is going down – you can switch into a money bond and ride out a bear market in tranquillity while your portfolio earns a healthy rate of interest on the money markets. (There is almost an exact correlation between bear markets and high money-market rates.) Most companies allow at least one or two free switches of this type in a year. Over this level there is a charge of ½ per cent to 1 per cent of the value of the units which are switched from one bond to another.

Be on your guard

The trouble with switching is that, until recently, there was no completely independent adviser you could turn to for advice as to when to switch between bonds in the same group – or between bonds offered by different groups. Another point to watch out for is that the Government could change its mind about the tax relief given to life assurance regular premiums. In effect, the Inland Revenue provides the investor with a subsidy. This relief is the most critical factor in enabling high yields to be offered. A change in the subsidy, or its abolition, would have a much greater effect on the bond business than would a change in the interest rate structure.

Building Society Bonds

Confusion abounds on the scene because the building societies also offer Building Society Bonds which compete with the single-premium bonds. While they have been around for ten years, Building Society Bonds are better referred to as Building Society Insurance-linked Schemes, and there are over 40 of them on the market.

Building societies also obtain the tax relief clawback from the Inland Revenue by being linked to insurance companies. Thus the money invested by way of premiums attracts the subsidy by being routed via an insurance company linked to a building society. The insurance company keeps around 5 per cent to 10 per cent of the premiums paid by the investor for life cover (normally 80 times the monthly premium) for administration and then pays the money over to the building society which, in turn, lends it out for house mortgages. Beware of the word 'guaranteed' in bond advertising. The yields advertised aren't guaranteed over a fixed period of time (if you buy gilts and hold them to maturity) but are only guaranteed to be at a rate of interest (normally 2 per cent) over the particular building society's share account rate which can move up and down with the prevailing level of interest rates.

It makes sense with any of these schemes, which are structured for ten years, to cash them in after four years to get the best yield. This is because the effect of the life insurance subsidy grows steadily less after four years and pulls down the yield. The element of life cover can also reduce the yields for the elderly, or for those in bad health, as higher premiums will be demanded in the light of the increased risk being taken on board by the life insurance company.

17

Eurobonds – a much neglected investment sector

How are your Eurobond holdings? If you're thinking: 'Euro-what?' note that, to the Frankfurt pork butcher or Belgian dentist, the 'Eurobond' is as familiar an investment sector, as say, unit trusts in this country. The 40 years of exchange control now ended mean that the Eurobond is still relatively unknown here. You should get to know it, whether you are a private investor with £5,000-plus to put aside (the minimum dealing amount in the Eurobond market) or you are deploying company investments in the United Kingdom or overseas.

The Eurobond is a 'bearer security', meaning that it guarantees anonymity to the buyer. Eurobonds also pay interest gross of tax with one trifling exception, which we'll come to in a moment. You can buy Eurobonds denominated in all the hard trading currencies – US and Canadian dollars, Swiss francs, Japanese yen, Euro-sterling (our very own petro-currency), Dutch guilders, German marks and several Middle Eastern currencies.

The Eurobond offers you the chance to take an anonymous tax-unpaid position for the tax evader buying via an overseas bank in foreign exchange in a security which also pays interest – and you can make capital appreciation in the foreign exchange as well. For example, anyone who held money in Swiss francs in the last decade did better, in terms of appreciation, than they would have done from an investment in gold, until the yellow metal went through the $400 mark, and the francs would have paid interest (unlike gold which yields no income).

Anyone can readily see that the Eurobond offers the black economy operator an opportunity to hoard cash away in a haven which makes no returns to the United Kingdom Inland Revenue, pays interest gross of tax, and offers the chance of capital appreciation (or loss) on the currency front. Those attractions have long been recognised by West European black economy operators who like to cut their tax liability by siphoning off untraceable cash into the enormous offshore Eurobond market.

Not that the Eurobond market is there solely to meet the requirements of black economy participants. The bulk of investors in this market tend to be the banks, large companies, pension funds and the like. They want to match cash inflows with investments of varying maturities (up to 10 and, exceptionally, 15 years on the European market); and they insist on allocating their funds across the investment sectors of the world's financial centres to provide high returns allied with good commercial prudence.

Mind you, the Inland Revenue in the United Kingdom was quick as a flash to wake up to the opportunities offered by the Eurobond market to tax dodgers once exchange controls were dropped in October 1979. Soon after that, the taxmen insisted that British companies making Eurobond issues from the United Kingdom must make interest payments *after* tax (this is the trifling exception to which we referred earlier).

The Inland Revenue's move was designed to stop United Kingdom residents from acquiring bearer bonds and failing to declare the interest received. This raised a storm of protest among people who issue Eurobonds and make a secondary market on which the bonds can (theoretically) be bought and sold at any time – these people being primarily the merchant banks and consortia banks of the City of London.

The storm didn't last long. The Eurobond issuers soon realised that they merely had to make greater use of non-British banks as paying agents, while British investors could, without a qualm, pay interest received into non-British bank accounts. Such dodges have helped to boost the outflow of funds from the United Kingdom (see Fig. 7).

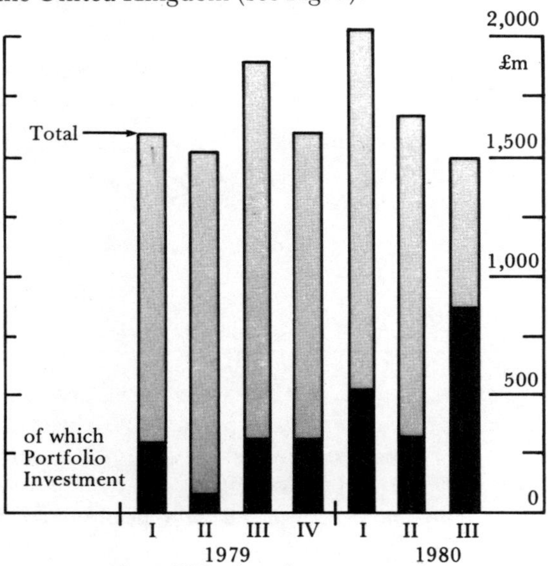

Fig. 7 UK private investment overseas.

For most of the period covered in Fig. 7, the outflow has been masked (and more than covered) by the heavy inflows of cash as a result of sterling's petrocurrency status and the high interest rates prevailing at that time.

Yes, but what is a Eurobond?

The way to think about Eurobonds, for a start, is that they fall somewhere between gilt-edged stock and large company loan stock. They are issued only by Governments, by large financial institutions and by multi-national companies with unquestioned credit rating (blue-chips in the United Kingdom, Triple-A rated in the USA).

They aren't as secure as gilts, though, because the vast Euromarkets (fuelled by enormous volumes of offshore hard currencies – primarily dollars) don't have a central bank, so there is no lender of last resort. If financial traumas really multiplied (which almost happened when Germany's Herstatt bank collapsed in the mid-1970s), the Euromarkets could conceivably crash – and provoke a catastrophe on the international money markets which would make the South Sea Bubble look like a soapsud!

As they are concerned that this might happen, the central banks are currently acting in concert to bring the Euromarkets under greater control. They are already huge. The Eurobond market swelled from $2.1 billion in 1974 to $14 billion in 1978. In 1979 it fell away to $10.5 billion because of the weakness in the dollar and economic recession which has reduced demand for bond issues, but that's still a massive amount.

Who issues the bonds? Table 12, showing the two years, 1978 and 1979, gives you the picture.

Table 12 Eurobond issues by category of borrower

$ billion	1978	1979
US companies	1.1	1.8
Foreign companies	4.5	3.8
State enterprises	3.3	2.7
Governments	3.6	1.3
International organisations	1.5	0.9
Total	14.0	10.5

It is a market offering an embarrassment of choice. Some 4,000 Eurobonds, denominated in every hard currency, have been pumped out by the large number of issuing banks which have jumped on the Eurobond bandwagon. They have earned fat fees (front-end commissions were 2 per cent to 2½ per cent in the fat years, but have been eroded in the leaner markets of 1979–83), but they have made a rod for their own backs in doing so.

The primary, or issuing market, has gone on gaily issuing more and more Eurobonds; but the secondary market – on which Eurobonds can be bought and sold – hasn't developed, and couldn't develop, at anything like the same rate. That's why private, or corporate, investors must make sure that the bonds they buy are of such undoubted quality in the eyes of the market that they can always be turned into cash in case of need.

In fact, many bond investors have lost money in the years when the US dollar was weak. Bond trading houses, too, were hit by losses when faced with the steep price decline of 1979 – and consequently in 1979/80 at least a third of all Eurobond issues had no secondary market.

The primary issuing market is growing as fast as the secondary market is contracting. It means that in buying a low-quality bond the investor runs the risk of being locked in for periods of up to 10 or 12 years until the bond matures and is redeemed. Banks with a good dealing reputation for Eurobonds include the Deutsche Bank, the Banque Nationale de Paris, Salomon Brothers (the New York investment bank), Merrill Lynch and Bank of America International. Remember that these banks are geared to the institutional, rather than the private, client. Barclays is the first British bank to start drawing the attention of private investors to Eurobonds and has issued a detailed brochure which is, in essence, a layman's guide to Eurobond investing.

Categories of Eurobonds

The 4,000 Eurobonds in issue can be grouped more conveniently into four categories. The biggest sector is the *fixed-rate*, or *straight* bonds. They have a fixed rate of interest and maturities of from three to 25 years and are similar to United Kingdom gilts.

Next come *floating-rate* notes, which have a fixed redemption date; but interest payments vary with prevailing interest rates – with the rate being pegged every six months as a fixed margin (say, 1.4 per cent) over the six months' London Interbank Offered Rate. So if interest rates are volatile it's a good idea to get the protection of floating rate notes behind you rather than going for the fixed rate bonds.

Then there are bonds with *detachable warrants* which entitle holders to buy shares in the company issuing the bonds at a price fixed at the time of the issue. Lastly there are *convertible bonds* which carry the right to convert the bond to shares at a fixed rate. For this conversion right, investors have to accept a slightly lower interest rate.

For the investor who wants to diversify part of his portfolio out of sterling, but who doesn't want the task of picking his way through the thousands of choices available, and making his appraisal of possible currency gains and comparative inflation rates country by country, there are a number of managed Eurobond funds available. For a fee (a front-end loading fee plus an annual management charge) these offshore funds (normally run from the Channel Islands) will manage the portion of your cash which you are willing to put into Eurobonds. On the other hand, if you prefer to deal direct, most London stockbrokers are equipped to advise on Eurobond purchases and offer dealing facilities, for a commission.

Some useful addresses if you want to put your money into offshore funds investing in Eurobonds are: 'Unibond', Barclays Unicorn International, 1 Charing Cross, St Helier, Jersey; Britannia International High Interest Fund, Britannia Trust Management (CI) Ltd, Trinity House, Bath Street, St Helier, Jersey; Sterling Bond Fund, Brown Shipley & Co, Channel House, Green Street, St Helier, Jersey; International Bond Fund, Gartmore, 1503 Hutchinson House, 10 Harcourt Road, Hong Kong.

18

Zero coupon and deep discount bonds – for capital gain only

Zero coupon bonds and deep discount bonds are aimed at investors seeking capital gain only – no income. They are issued by companies which can claim the notional interest rate on the bond against tax. The other advantage of the bonds is that they relieve the company issuing them from the burden of servicing debt interest charges year by year as no, or little, interest is actually paid to the bond holder.

Until 1981, when the zero bonds made a major impact on the US and Eurobond scene, companies issuing bonds used the traditional route of fixing a rate of interest high enough to ensure the issue was taken up by their issuing bank's clients – whether corporate investors (pension funds, insurance companies) or private individuals. The bond could be issued at a reasonable discount to the redemption price to provide a capital gain. For example a bond issued at £95 would be redeemed in ten years' time at £100. These two factors – the rate of interest and the size of the discount – were the key factors in the minds of bond-issuing banks in the City of London, New York and other financial centres round the world, allied to the security offered by the borrower. The right combination meant that the bonds were taken up in full, the issuing bank thereby earning its issuing commission and enhancing its reputation.

There are many investors who don't want income at all – particularly if that income is taxed (and even more so if the income is taxed at the unearned income rate once the investment income surcharge comes into play). Greed creating a need, the zero coupon bond has been introduced to cater for the non-income seekers. Typically, the zero coupon bond, if issued in the United Kingdom, would have a face value of £100 and be redeemed at that price in between 7 and 15 years, depending on the redemption date chosen by the issuing company. The company pays no interest during the years, but, instead, the 'notional' interest rate would be set to produce, say, a 15 per cent a year return, but the investor gets it 'rolled up' on redemption. To allow for the interest, the issue price at the outset is set at, say £24.50 per £100 nominal (a massive discount). The issue price is also calculated to allow for (theoretic) reinvestment opportunities from the nominal interest for the investor.

From the company point of view, the advantages of the zero coupon bond is that it doesn't have to service the debt by heavy yearly interest charges. For example, Barclays made a 16 per cent domestic bond issue in the United Kingdom a few years ago to raise 20-year money when interest rates were at high levels. That 16 per cent produced anguished cries from the Association of Treasurers who felt that, in setting the rate at such a high level, Barclays was spoiling the bond market for other operators. Contrast that 16 per cent with the Barclays zero coupon bond, issued in the USA through Barclays' American Corporation.

Non taxpaying bodies – such as sovereign states – can use the zero coupon strategy by tapping into the Eurobond market and lowering their interest burden 'at a stroke'. The problem for the British investor (who is perfectly free to buy US domestic, or Euro, zero-rated bonds as there are no exchange controls) is that the Inland Revenue has stubbornly stuck to its policy of symmetry that companies can offset the normal interest against their tax bills year. On the other hand, investors must treat the notional income, as income, year by year, thus removing the whole capital gain 'roll up' at a stroke.

For example, if a British investor decided to hedge out of sterling by taking up US zero-rated bonds (which would give him his eventual gain in dollars in seven or ten years' time) a good deal of the gilt on this particular piece of gingerbread would be removed as the 'gain' is taxed not as capital gain (which offers index linking and indexed thresholds) but as income.

The problem for the United Kingdom Government is that it is in a privileged position as a borrower which has weakened its position in arguing against those with private sector companies which want the same privileges. In an effort to lower the crippling interest charges on Government borrowing via the gilt market, the (then) Chancellor decided to widen the concept of indexation from the National Savings sector (index-linked certificates, SAYE) to the gilt market. Instead of just offering indexed-linked gilts to pension fund managers (who didn't greatly like them because they didn't provide the running income which pension funds need, and also because traditional gilts were offering a real return over and above the UK rate of inflation) the Chancellor offered index-linked gilts to all and sundry. The first 'people's' gilt was an issue of £750 million of 2 per cent indexed-linked Treasury Stock 1988 with both the capital and interest elements linked to the Retail Prices Index – and there have been many more indexed gilts issued.

There is no capital gains tax on gilts held for over one year, including the indexed-linked gilts and the low coupon 'surtax' payer's gilts which offer little in the way of income but assured capital gain if held to maturity. Hence the potency of the argument 'why should the Government be the only privileged borrower to tap the savings market in this way?' Why shouldn't large British companies and financial institutions – as companies can in the USA or via the Eurobond market – tap the vast UK market by way of domestic bond issues aimed at investors who don't want income but only the assurance of capital gain? (A gain which, furthermore, would be taxed *as* capital gain and not income.) Some freedom to do this has been granted. British companies can now issue zero coupon and deep discount bonds, but the Inland Revenue's tax treatment means they are unattractive to private investors.

And the 'zero warrants'?

For the really speculative investor, the zero bond markets have also spun off their own high risk sector by way of zero coupon warrants. A number of US companies issuing zero coupon bonds also issue warrants with them. These give the investor the right to subscribe for more of the bonds in the future on the basis of a predetermined redemption yield. This offers the risk-taking investor the opportunity to bet on a future fall in interest rates. As the latter falls away, the value of warrants (which gives the holder the right to buy himself a higher return than offered by the markets) increases. Not only does the intrinsic value of the warrant increase, but it also gives the buyer 'gearing up' opportunities. One warrant can give the buyer the right to buy many times that number of underlying securities, the warrants being traded separately to the 'parent' bonds.

A typical zero Eurobond may provide the speculator with, say, 100 warrants which buys him the right to buy $100,000 worth of bonds. For example, the Fluor Corporation warrants could be bought for $2,000 per 100 in 1982 in London via a broker or bank. Then the market woke up to the fact that the six or so zero coupon bond warrants traded in London had short lives (they were due to expire between August and December 1982). This resulted in a rise in Fluor's warrant price from $20 to $32 in the autumn of 1982 in a short space of time, so the $2,000 invested quickly translated itself into $3,200. And at this price 100 Fluor warrants give the right to buy $100,000 nominal of Fluor's zero coupon bonds at a guaranteed yield to maturity of 14 per cent. If you strip out the cost of the warrants, this brings down the return to 13.18 per cent. If interest rates tumble to, say, the 10 per cent level (which happened in 1983) the value of the warrants rises to $12,800 presenting the lucky holder with a windfall capital gain. If rates were to rise to 20 per cent, the value of the warrants would reduce in the same proportion. But the outlay on the warrants is comparatively slight, and there is a two and a half year time scale during which time anything can happen.

Watch out, by the way, for forgeries in the zero coupon bond sector. One enterprising forger got away with millions in 1983 by forging zero coupon bonds for the J. C. Penney Corporation on the principle that, as the bonds paid no interest, the certificates would be put away for years and the risk of detection was slight. The forgery was spotted quickly – but only by accident!

19

Investing surplus cash in sterling

One of the most important lessons which has emerged from the volatile investment scene of the last decade is the necessity of keeping a 'cash cushion' which is available quickly for emergency needs. The requirement to keep a percentage (10, or 20, per cent) of one's investment portfolio in short-term 'homes' which are easily accessible is greater for those who have retired and whose pensions have kept pace with inflation – particularly with rates, electricity, gas bills, etc., rising remorselessly.

Sensible deployment of this cash cushion is just as important as deploying one's portfolio for the longer term – in shares, gilts, property and the rest. Yet most people tend to be somewhat lazy about putting their surplus cash where it will earn maximum interest – and that extra interest could go towards paying unexpectedly high bills.

There is little sense in leaving more in one's current account with a clearing bank than is necessary to avoid paying bank charges, plus having enough available to draw on for living expenses. You pay bank charges on your current account if your credit balance falls below a set minimum – normally £100 – at any time (even if only for one day) during the three months' bank 'charging' period. The charges are calculated after deducting a notional allowance on the average credit balance from total charges, dependent on the number of debit transactions (see Table 13). The trouble with keeping too much money in a current account is that it earns the holder no interest, although it provides the 'Big Four' clearing banks (Barclays, National Westminster, Lloyds and Midland) with useful extra profits because the banks can put this 'free' money to good, profitable use.

While no member of the 'Big Four' clearing banks offers interest on current account money, some banks are experimenting with schemes (sometimes involving a cheque book facility) which pay interest on regular monthly deposits, such as the Lloyds Cash Flow Account. The Midland is

Table 13 1983 bank charges

Bank	Minimum for free banking	Charges when account falls below minimum Cheque	Cash machine	Standing order	Direct debit	Notional interest
Barclays	£100	28p	28p	28p	15p	3 per cent
Lloyds	£100	27½p	20p	27½p	20p	2½ per cent
Midland	£100	28p	15p	28p	15p	1½ per cent
National Westminster*	£100	29p	12p	29p	12p	3 per cent
Co-op	Nil	30p	–	30p	30p	Nil
National Girobank	Nil	30p†	–	30p†	30p†	Nil
TSB	£100	15p	10p	15p	15p	Nil
Williams & Glyn's	Nil	29p‡	14p	14p	14p‡	3 per cent
Yorkshire	Nil	25p	18p	25p	18p	2½ per cent
Bank of Scotland	£50	22p	15p	15p	15p	3 per cent
Clydesdale	Nil	23p	15p	30p	15p	3½ per cent
Royal Bank of Scotland	£50	23p	16p	26p	16p	2¾ per cent
TSB Scotland	Nil	15p	15p	15p	15p	Nil

* Plus £3 a quarter if you pay other charges.
† Only while overdrawn.
‡ Also for credits.

also becoming involved in this area, along with the Bank of Scotland. The trouble with switching current account surplus cash to the same bank's deposit account is that the rate offered by the clearing banks on seven-day deposit funds is normally lower than can be obtained elsewhere.

Faced with this low yield, the basic rate taxpayer has the alternative of putting his, or her, surplus cash in a building society where a (normally) higher return can be obtained. It is important to realise that building societies are only suitable for basic rate taxpayers because basic rate tax is deducted at source and no machinery exists for the investor, not liable to basic rate tax, to reclaim tax from the Inland Revenue. For this reason, the building societies (which have a substantial number of investors, many of them retired and not liable to any tax) themselves pay a composite rate of tax of 25¼ per cent. This is well below the 30 per cent basic rate of tax because, every four years, the Inland Revenue checks a sample of building society investors to assess how many investors are not liable to tax at all, and each year they, and the Building Societies Association, negotiate the composite rate. The composite rate could drop further if personal allowances are increased faster than the rate of inflation and more people drop out of the tax net altogether.

There are also the 'money funds' – Simco, Tyndall, the United Dominions Trust average rate fund, the Schroder funds, Save & Prosper and others – into which surplus cash can be placed for short periods, the funds taking anything from £1,000 and upwards, to, in the case of UDT, a £5,000 minimum deposit. Such money funds are extremely popular in the

USA and, now also, in the United Kingdom owing to the 'ceilings' which were placed on bank deposit interest levels.

In essence the United Kingdom money funds operate in much the same way as the US money funds. The United Kingdom funds 'pool' the investments of a number of small depositors and on-lend the money to the vast wholesale sterling money markets of the city – the interbank market, the local authority money market and the inter-company money market. The existence of these money funds enables small depositors to get wholesale money market rates, but it's worth noting that those with £10,000 or £20,000 surplus to requirements can get the wholesale money market rates direct by way of a 'special deposit' via their clearing bank.

Some of the money funds on offer are listed in Table 14.

Table 14 Some money funds on offer

Tyndall Demand Fund: Minimum deposit – £2,500. Interest paid quarterly.
Tyndall Seven-day Fund: Minimum deposit – £2,500. Interest credited quarterly. Chequebook provided.
Simco Call Fund: Minimum deposit – £25,000. Interest paid annually.
Simco Seven-day Fund: Minimum deposit – £1,000. Interest paid half yearly.
Mallinhall Call Deposit Fund: Minimum deposit – £5,000. Interest paid quarterly or annually.
Save & Prosper's High Interest Fund: Mimimum deposit – £2,500. No formal distribution dates. Chequebook provided.
Western Trust and Savings One Month Notice Account: Minimum deposit – £2,500. Interest paid monthly.
Schroder Seven-day Account: Minimum deposit – £2,500. Interest paid half yearly.
United Dominions Trust Average Rate Account: Minimum deposit – £5,000. Interest paid quarterly.
Tullett & Riley Money Market Trust: comprising: Call Fund (sums available on demand) and Seven-day Fund. Minimum deposit in Call fund is £10,000, and in Seven-day Fund – £2,500. Interest credited daily.

20

Investing surplus cash in foreign currency deposits and offshore currency funds

Foreign currency deposits

If you had had the sense to put your surplus cash into a US dollar account when sterling was worth \$2.42 back in 1980, you would have made a large capital gain by the time sterling dropped to \$1.45 in 1983 – and earned interest on the deposit throughout, interest which at times approached the 19 per cent mark. It would have provided you with a much bigger return than leaving the cash in sterling. Of course the bulk of the gain came from the decline in sterling against the dollar. Bear in mind that you can lose to the same extent if sterling rose against the dollar or any other hard currency – Swiss francs, Japanese yen, Deutschmarks – in which you can make a foreign currency deposit on an 'at call' basis. This deposit is repayable whenever you want it – for seven days, a month, two months, all the way through to one year and even longer.

The clearing banks have been carrying out a brisk business in opening foreign currency accounts for United Kingdom residents ever since the pound's honeymoon period in 1980 started to cease and sterling slid steadily compared with most other hard currencies. Note that, in opening a foreign currency account your cash is then pushed out by the bank in question on to the Eurocurrencies deposit market. The bank takes a 'turn' on the rate of interest it can get for US dollars, Swiss francs, Deutschmarks, or even Eurosterling, and the rate it offers you. Small depositors, with around £1,000, can expect to get 2 per cent or 3 per cent less than the interest rates offered for large amounts of £100,000 or more. The bank also makes a 'turn' for itself on the exchange transaction.

For this reason it is well worth shopping around between the banks to see if you can improve on the terms offered – certainly so far as the interest rate is concerned. Of course, it is perfectly legal to open a foreign currency account via an overseas bank, located, for example, in Switzerland. This is

a favourite ploy of many people who have income which has not been declared for tax and wish to place the money with a bank which has no reporting requirements to the United Kingdom Inland Revenue (British banks and all foreign banks in the United Kingdom must report on any interest paid gross of over £15 per annum).

A favourite route is to open a Swiss fiduciary account which means that all the cash is invested outside Switzerland, usually on the Eurocurrencies deposit market. This provides a higher yield, plus prospective capital gain if you choose the right currencies into which to deposit your offshore cash, than investing in the Swiss domestic market which provides a low interest return as a rule. However, the costs of operating Swiss bank fiduciary accounts can be high, so this should be checked out first.

For many a tax avoider, the USA offers a common language and a large selection of banks (over 2,000 banks), plus the mutual funds (akin to the United Kingdom money funds). However, US banks do report any deposit made with them of over $10,000 to the American Internal Revenue Service and any interest paid gross of tax of over $20. With the age of computer matching with us, there are many who reckon that the Inland Revenues of the United Kingdom and United States will co-operate to spot tax dodgers on both sides of the Atlantic.

The offshore currency funds

As an alternative to keeping surplus cash on the United Kingdom mainland or opening a United Kingdom-based foreign currency deposit account, the investor has the option of transferring cash to one of the many offshore currency funds based mainly in the Channel Islands.

The concept of the funds is simple enough. For a United Kingdom investor to make a currency deposit with his own bank – unless he has over £100,000 to deposit – entails not only taking the inevitable exchange rate risk, but also getting a poor deal as you've seen above. The rate of interest offered may be 2 per cent or 3 per cent less than the wholesale rate of interest the bank will get by on-lending the deposit into the Eurocurrencies market. The exchange rate given for swapping the sterling deposit unto US dollars, Deutschmarks, Swiss francs, or the other 'hard' trading currencies which make up the Eurocurrencies deposit market, will not be particularly good. The offshore funds take in the deposits from investors and, by pooling them, can get the best wholesale rates of interest offered for the various currencies by the Eurocurrencies deposit market, and also get the best rate of exchange.

All the investor has to do is to decide, unless he invests via a managed currency fund, which currency, or which currencies, will stand to make him the best capital gain against sterling. He can keep his funds in sterling which is then invested on the Eurosterling deposit market.

The investor does not, in fact, buy a currency deposit. What he does buy is shares in the fund relating to the particular currency of his choice. The reason why the inflow of cash into the funds reached such epic proportions during 1982 and 1983 was not only because sterling slid alarmingly, and the funds offered a hedging opportunity against this slide, but also because of the tax situation.

The funds offered investors the opportunity of rolling up interest earned on the deposit (which would normally be paid out by way of dividend on the shares in the fund and taxed as such) into capital gain. Hence they were termed 'roll up' funds. Potentially highly taxed income was rolled up into the appreciating value of the shares. Capital gains tax (given the exemptions) was only payable when the investor finally cashed in his shares in the funds. Swaps inside the funds from one currency's shares to another were also made on a capital gains tax-free basis until the investor cashed his shares in finally.

The funds' ability to turn potentially highly taxed interest into nil, or low, taxed capital gain was so attractive to high rate taxpayers and the Inland Revenue was so worried as to the sheer volume (£1.5 billion) which moved into the funds, that the Chancellor of the Exchequer decided to remove some of the attractions in autumn 1983. He removed the facility to 'roll up' income into capital gain although he allowed a period of grace until 1 January 1984. Until that date, investors in the funds faced only a capital gains tax liability rather than an income tax liability as is now the case. Nevertheless the currency funds continue to offer some tax advantages. The tax charge falls only when the investor withdraws cash from the funds. This means that the high tax payer awaiting retirement (when the marginal rate of tax may drop) can 'roll up' his income until retirement by using the facility of the funds.

As you can see from Table 15, the funds tend to be the offspring of the City's merchant banking community. The managers sit in Jersey or Guernsey, but the foreign exchange decisions are made in the City by banks which run big foreign exchange dealing departments. Typically, the funds will offer shares in at least five currencies – the US dollar, sterling, the Swiss franc, the Deutschmark and the Japanese yen, although one fund, Rothschild's Old Court, offers ten currencies. Management commissions vary from around the ¾ per cent mark up to 5 per cent, although this latter figure is normally charged by funds such as Hill Samuel which throw in a currency management service. This means you don't have to make your own buying and selling decisions; the fund managers will make them for you. The funds which charge small management commissions tend to be of the type which cater for the investor making his own decision as to which currency to buy, although, if you have enough funds on deposit (for example, £100,000 in the case of Rothschild's Old Court) a fund management service may be supplied.

There are detailed variations between the funds. Some funds are really in the nature of offshore bank deposits, and are primarily aimed at companies with large sums to deposit, which want quick withdrawal terms and

Table 15 The main currency funds

Fund	Manager
Dollar-managed Currency Fund	Britannia International Investment Management Ltd, Box 271, Queensway House, Queen St, St Helier, Jersey (Tel: 0534 73114).
Sterling-managed Currency Fund	Britannia International Investment Management Ltd.
International Currency Fund	Brown Shipley Trust Company (Jersey) Ltd, P.O. Box 583, St Helier, Jersey (Tel. 0534 74777).
The Currency Trust	Capital Asset Managers, Bermuda House, St Julian's Avenue, St Peter Port, Guernsey (Tel. 0481 26268).
Central Assets Currency Funds Ltd	Charterhouse Japhet Currency Management Ltd, Channel House, St Helier, Jersey (Tel. 0534 74689).
Guinness Mahon International Fund (Guernsey)	P.O. Box 188, St Peter Port, Guernsey (Tel. 0481 23506).
International Currency Fund	Hill Samuel Investment Management Ltd, P.O. Box 63, Jersey (Tel. 0534 76029).
Managed Fund	Hill Samuel Investment Management Ltd.
Leopold Joseph & Sons International Fund	Leopold Joseph & Sons (Guernsey), Hirzel Court, St Peter Port, Guernsey (Tel. 0481 26648).
International Currency Fund	Phoenix International, P.O. Box 77, St Peter Port, Guernsey (Tel. 0481 26741).
International Currency Fund	Providence Capitol International Ltd, P.O. Box 121, St Peter Port, Guernsey (Tel. 0481 26726/9).
Old Court International Reserves Ltd	Rothschild Asset Management (CI), P.O. Box 58, St Julians Court, Guernsey (Tel. 0481 26741).
RBC International Currencies Fund Ltd	Royal Bank of Canada Investment Managers Ltd, P.O. Box 246, St Julian's Court, Guernsey (Tel. 0481 23021).
Multicurrency Reserve Fund	Save & Prosper International, P.O. Box 246, St Peter Port, Guernsey (Tel. 0481 23021).
Managed Currency Fund	Schroder Unit Trust Managers International Ltd, P.O. Box 273, St Peter Port, Guernsey (Tel. 0481 28750).
Vanbrugh Currency Fund	Vanbrugh Fund Management International Ltd, 28–34 Hill St, St Helier, Jersey (Tel. 0534 36281).
Citifunds	Citibank (Channel Islands) Ltd, Channel House, P.O. Box 104, Green St, St Helier, Jersey (Tel. 0534 70334).
County Bank Currency Fund	National Westminster Bank, 23–25 Broad Street, St Helier, Jersey (Tel. 0534 70041).

economic currency switching facilities. Some, like Old Court, will accept quite small sums from private investors.

Other funds are structured more like unit trusts. An example is Guinness Mahon's International Fund. This is a managed fund, so that investors leave it to the advisers to decide which currencies should be held by the fund. To give an example, just before the General Election of 1983, the fund's cash was invested as to 40 per cent in sterling, 25 per cent in Deutschmarks and 20 per cent in US dollars.

Some funds offer two choices. Citifunds, an off-shoot of Citibank, offers investors a choice between individual holdings in sterling, dollars, Deutschmarks, Swiss francs or yen and makes a 1 per cent management charge. Alternatively they can invest in a managed fund, which is more expensive with a 2 per cent annual charge and a 2½ per cent front-end charge for investments under $10,000. The higher level of charges mean that the managed fund should be viewed as more in the nature of a longer term investment. It involves having faith in the skill of the managers who will aim to make the most of exchange rate and interest rate swings.

Alternatively, the investor can choose other types of foreign currency funds on offer overseas or in the United Kingdom. One such is BIA Bond Investments – a Swiss bond fund based in a low tax Swiss canton which could turn out to be more profitable if an investment currency premium was ever to re-appear after the re-imposition of United Kingdom exchange controls. BIA Bond Investments can be contacted at EBS (Management) Ltd, 38 Finsbury Square, London EC2A 1PX (Tel. 01-588 1932) and at 10 Baarerstrasse, 6301 Zug, Switzerland (Tel. 042.21.71.80).

Investing in BIA does mean you must have faith that the Swiss franc will go on steadily increasing in value against the pound, which has certainly been the lesson of the last decade. Swiss franc interest rates tend to be notoriously low so most of the potential capital gain must come from the fall in the pound against the Swiss franc. BIA pursues a highly conservative investment policy in putting out its cash on the Swiss market.

21

Commodity investment – a case of *caveat emptor*

The Latin tag *caveat emptor* (let the buyer beware) holds particularly true when it comes to commodity investment. One or two well publicised scandals have brought home to many potential investors on the commodity markets the fact that unscrupulous brokers, particularly when dealing with the vagaries of highly volatile markets, can produce nasty losses. It is estimated that over 80 per cent of private investors speculating in commodities end up losing money. In a court case in 1983, Mr Justice Bax claimed that the world of commodity dealing was a 'jungle' where small animals (investors) are the most vulnerable prey.

Commodity dealing is a highly risky business, even with the most respectable companies, let alone the more dubious brokers who offer the promise of large profits which can very quickly turn into even larger losses. Commodity speculation is not for the small investor because the odds are stacked so heavily against him. Buying the actual metal, or commodity, is, for the outsider, either impractical or costly. Storage, maintaining quality and insurance are just some of the problems. Obviously small quantities of precious metals can be bought from dealers, such as gold, silver or platinum, but the prices charged by the dealers for small quantities will be heavily loaded and the 'spread' between the amount charged by the dealer when selling and buying back is often very wide because the dealer can dictate terms.

Little regulation

There are very few rules and regulations governing the activities of commodity brokers who often solicit aggressively for business from the general public. Before October 1979, the Bank of England used the foreign exchange control schemes, which commodity companies had to join, as a means of forcing members of the exchanges to provide the detailed reports needed to monitor the markets effectively. Since then this practice has been reduced to a passive, informal, watchdog role, relying purely on voluntary self-regulation by members of the exchanges with the help of the International Commodities Clearing House, now owned by the clearing banks. While this works well, and flexibly, there is little protection for outside participants in the markets – no compensation fund, no body to handle complaints and no restrictions on anyone setting himself up as a commodity broker handling money from the public.

The main danger area is not to be found among the properly run companies, which are members of the London exchanges and are punctilious in ensuring speculators are aware of the high risks involved (to the point at which they will turn away small investors), but in the next tier down. This is the tier comprising the fringe, or bucket shop operators, who have few scruples and often concentrate on the smaller investors as the established brokers don't want to deal with them. There is considerable scope for unscrupulous brokers to mislead or exploit the unsuspecting public who have little redress under existing law. The Department of Trade, under outdated legislation conceived for a different purpose, does ban the promotion of commodity syndicates or unauthorised offshore funds, but there are many loopholes which can be used, such as seminars and press articles and aggressive marketing tactics.

Dealing direct

It is generally agreed by London commodity brokers that a minimum of between £5,000 to £10,000 of 'risk' capital, which the client can afford to lose without hardship, is required before he can even contemplate direct commodity investment using the futures market. Some companies require a great deal more. The first move is to get a reputable broker who is a member of one of the following:

London Commodity Exchange, Cereal House, 58 Mark Lane, London EC3.

London Metal Exchange, Plantation House, Fenchurch Street, London EC3.

London Gold Futures Market, 3rd Floor, East Wing, Plantation House, London EC3.

London Grain and Feed Trade Association, Baltic Exchange Chambers, 24–28 St Mary Axe, London EC3.

Even when using a reputable broker, bear in mind that many employees of reputable broking houses are paid on the business they generate so they have a vested interest in 'churning' (persuading the client to overtrade in order to increase the commissions).

Having picked a broker, the investor has two choices. One is to hand over his cash to be managed by him. This is a 'discretionary account' which has the advantage of relieving the investor of making his own decisions. However, this sort of account can be taken advantage of if the broker is unscrupulous.

Alternatively, the client makes his own decisions when and what to buy and sell, and can take advice from the broker or disregard it. The latter 'trading account' means you have to monitor the commodity markets yourself and can take advantage of the 'gearing effect'. This comes from dealing on the commodities' futures market which means that you have to put down 10 per cent of the face value of the futures contract so your capital has ten times its buying power. This enables you to take up a relatively large number of positions in commodities on a limited amount of capital. However, you have to be prepared to make available additional cash so that you can top up your margins when the market goes against you.

The doctrine of unlimited liability prevails in direct dealing of this type (unlike the discretionary account in which, in theory at least, once you hand over your initial cash, that is the full amount of your liability). You, the client, bear all the risks and indemnify the broker in the event of a default on your account.

The gearing up effect or 'leverage' is where the dangers lie. The attraction is that, say, £10,000 can be used to speculate in futures worth £100,000, meaning that big profits can be made for a small outlay. It also magnifies, in the same way, the losses which can be suffered, hence the many stories of unsuspecting commodity speculators 'losing their shirts'. It is not realised generally that the margin, charged essentially to protect the broker from client losses, has to be topped up continually if prices move against the investor. It is not appreciated often that, in order to retain the original margin, the client has to pay up to 100 per cent of the losses incurred. These can add up alarmingly quickly in fast moving markets.

If the margin is not topped up immediately on request, the broker instantly closes the position out, using the margin money to cover losses suffered. This is why so many small investors may guess the long-term trend in a commodity correctly but may be wiped out by unpredictable short term fluctuations, simply because they haven't got sufficient resources. One way to tackle the problem is to be very disciplined in your trading and cut your losses quickly. Another is to use a recognised trading system and stick to it rigidly. Many speculators rely on computer systems or charts to make their decisions, however these aren't guarantees against losing money and they do require tremendous discipline and an endless supply of money.

Or the options route

Another method is to speculate via options. This is safer in that the amount of risk is limited to the premium paid for an option to buy or sell a futures contract at a known price. Instead of buying a commodity contract you can buy a commodity option at the cost of paying a premium. The option can be taken up or abandoned, depending on whether the commodity price moves in the right or wrong direction.

A 'call option' gives you the right to buy, at an agreed price, any time between the day you buy the option and the date it expires. It is a suitable method to use if you think the market will rise. A 'put option' gives you the right to sell at an agreed price at any time between the day you buy the option and the date it expires. This tactic can be used if you think the market will go down. A 'double option' works both ways (not, however, at the same time) but you have to pay twice the call or put option premiums.

Generally speaking, the premium you pay for an option is determined by the length of time the options has to run and the state of the market at the time you are buying. Normally the premium will be higher the longer the period of the option and the more volatile the market. As a rough guide the premium will normally be in the range of 5 per cent to 15 per cent of the market value of the contract. Bear in mind that the price of the commodity has to rise (or fall) enough to provide you with a capital gain over and above the cost of the option.

Essentially the buyer of a non-transferable option which is favoured in London starts at a disadvantage by 'losing' the premium which has to be made up via capital gain. The investor has to be very careful about premiums paid since there are no officially published rates, so check with several brokers as to option premiums.

The commodity fund route

A less risky approach is to use the commodity fund route. These are funds based offshore or onshore. The lowest risk category of all are the UK-based unit trusts which deal in commodity-related company shares – legislation prevents them from owning commodities directly. When gold is rising, unit trusts like Target Gold and Britannia Gold & General come into their own on the back of their investments in gold mines and mining finance houses. This tends to produce a better performance than the actual metal prices – and the reverse is true if prices go down. The same goes for commodity and energy trusts such as Midland Bank Commodity & General, Gartmore Energy and National Westminster Energy. Overall, there are about 25 unit trusts in the 'national resources' sector – one of the oldest and best being Hambro Metals and Minerals. An investment of £1,000 in 1975 would have grown to £3,200 by the end of 1982.

And the offshore funds

The offshore, 'unauthorised' funds are based in tax havens and trade in physical commodities, or more likely in the futures markets where a good fund manager can make the most of large resources and the leverage available. The volatility of the markets and the leverage involve high risk in return for the chance of high reward. The small private investor can take a stake in such a fund for a relatively modest outlay and most funds guarantee that the investor is only liable for the amount initially put up, but this should be checked. The great advantage of such funds lies in taxation – the speculator has a much greater chance of paying only capital gainst tax, since he is basically investing in shares, not in the commodities (the Inland Revenue can attack a 'physical' trader by treating capital gains as income).

Even among the offshore funds there are some which pursue more risky investment policies than others. An example of a large, middle of the road (in terms of risk) fund is Old Court Commodity Fund (run by Rothschild's via Old Court Commodity Fund Managers). A fund which is active on the futures market, for example, is the CAL Metals Fund, based in the Isle of Man and backed by chartist David Fuller's Commodity Analysis.

Overall, the offshore funds need to be treated with caution by the investor who should be fully aware of the risks he is taking with his money. Check whether the funds are 'open ended' – meaning that you can buy and sell your shares in the fund at any time – and check the charging system of the fund management company. The system whereby the managers' reward for their services is geared to the financial weight of the big investors can work to the disadvantage of the small investor – so read the small print. Remember that commodity investment is no different from any other investment market. Success is all a matter of timing and capital gains come from getting in somewhere near the bottom and getting out near the top. Not many can do this – so be content with a reasonable gain and take your profits.

22

Investing in 'bullion' gold coins

'Bullion' gold coins have a nice, piratical ring to them. Yet they defy their name. They are not 'pieces of eight' dug up from treasure caches in the West Indies. They are coins produced in modern times by the South Africans, the Canadians, the Russians and the British to satisfy those investors who like to keep a proportion of their wealth in gold, but in the form of coins rather than in gold bar. They are called 'bullion' gold coins by the London Gold Market to differentiate them from the numismatic, or collectors', gold coins. The difference between the two types of coins is that bullion gold coins have prices which move roughly in relation to the price of gold on the world market, with a premium over and above the intrinsic gold content varying from coin to coin. The prices of numismatic gold coins are not tied in the same way to the world gold price, although their value is obviously influenced by it. Their value depends on scarcity, or rarity, age and condition, and they constitute a totally different market from that of bullion gold coins.

The British and gold coins

To understand the workings of the bullion gold coin market it is worth looking into its background. From the outbreak of the Second World War until 1954 the London Gold Market was closed. Between 1954 and April 1971 the 'Rule of Four' prevailed so far as buying gold coins was concerned. Under this rule it wasn't possible for United Kingdom residents to buy gold coins without the specific consent of the Bank of England, and even when this consent was given they were limited to a prescribed number – four – of each specimen. The 'Rule of Four' was designed to ensure that scarce foreign exchange would be confined to meeting the needs of bona fide collectors.

Not that speculators were missing very much for the majority of the years from 1939 to 1971. You have to remember that the price of gold was kept artificially low for a very long period of time – a period in which an investment in a four-bedroom house would have far outstripped gold so far as capital gain was concerned.

During the nineteenth century, pound notes were freely converted into gold and were – albeit fractionally – backed by gold, hence the term 'the gold standard'. At the same time, private currency issues by commercial banks became increasingly rare and central banks (in the case of the United Kingdom, the Bank of England) took over a steadily increasing share of the responsibility for our paper currency until it achieved a total monopoly eventually. In August 1914, while the lights were going out over Europe, the gold standard was suspended, never to be restored fully, although in 1925 a modified gold standard, known as the 'gold bullion standard' (so called because gold coins, such as the sovereign, were no longer in circulation) was reintroduced and lasted, with somewhat disastrous results for employment, until 1931.

The 'Rule of Four' was lifted in April 1971 and United Kingdom residents were free to buy as many gold coins – but not gold bullion in bar form – as they wanted. The lifting of the restriction came at a time, 1973–74, when the gold price was starting to soar to (at that time) unprecedented levels as investors world-wide invested in gold, deserting shares, bonds, gilt-edged stocks in the face of rip roaring inflation, currency turmoil and the aftermath of the first OPEC oil price explosion. Gold coins looked to the British – who were at that time denied the opportunity of buying gold in bar form – as a good way of protecting part of their investments. The French bourgeoisie and peasantry had felt like that throughout the century and merely added to their existing stocks of gold 'Napoleons' kept under floorboards or in family bank deposit boxes.

In Britain coin dealers mushroomed overnight – and many decamped equally quickly. The flight into gold attracted the television producers and in one memorable programme on the activities of a (then) major coin dealer, the camera focussed on an attractive girl sitting on the floor of a bedroom in a West End flat in London, shovelling gold coins into plastic containers. When asked what her job was she replied that she constituted a dealer's 'Despatch Department'. Her qualifications? She turned out to be an ex-Bunny girl.

Quite apart from the lunatic fringe of the coin-dealing industry, at least one of Britain's major clearing banks recorded a private individual walking into one of its Sheffield branches and placing a single order for £250,000 worth of krugerrands. The flood of British investors into gold coins, particularly South African krugerrands, caused the Chancellor of the Exchequer of the time, Denis Healey, to clamp down in his April 1975 Budget. 'The time has come,' he announced to the House of Commons, to stop this drain [the cost in foreign exchange of gold coins coming in from abroad] which has amounted to, on average, £25 million a month in the first quarter of this year.' Mind you, at that time sterling wasn't underpinned by North Sea oil and had not attained the desirable status which it now has as one of the world's petrocurrencies.

The net result was to bar gold coin imports and to create a domestic pool of coins while, at the same time, the Bank of England announced an end to new sovereign sales to United Kingdom residents. This created a two-tier market in gold coins in the United Kingdom – the domestic market and the international market. The domestic market was constituted by a pool of coins – principally krugerrands and sovereigns – which were bought by United Kingdom residents before the stable door was firmly bolted. The pool was static, as it couldn't be added to by imports or by minting new sovereigns. The only coins available for sale were those which were made available by other United Kingdom residents.

Full freedom

By June 1979, in one of the most radical Budgets of the century, the Chancellor of the Exchequer of the newly elected Conservative Government, scrapped the two-tier market system and gave full freedom to United Kingdom residents to buy as many gold coins as they wished. After all, by this time, the pound had produced a miraculous turn round from being one of the weakest of the world's trading currencies and was well on its way to becoming one of the strongest. Already the handlers of international hot money flows ('footloose' cash) were scenting the fact that, backed by North Sea oil, Britain's Balance of Payments with the rest of the world was going to move inevitably into the black – having been in the red on the trading account (excluding invisible earnings such as banking and insurance) for all but three of the preceding 100 years or so. Remember hot money flows to currencies where there is little downside risk and a better-than-average chance of capital appreciation.

The scrapping of the Healey two-tier market came as no relief to the coin smugglers who were in prison. By putting a barrier on gold coin imports and creating a two-tier market in, for example, krugerrands, a profitable operation could be carried out by buying krugerrands at the (lower) international price in Western Europe and smuggling them in to Britain for sale at the (higher) domestic price. This lasted from April 1975 to June 1979, but still the British could only buy gold coins – not gold bars. The final freedom came on 23 October 1979 when Sir Geoffrey Howe not only abolished the exchange controls which had been in force since 25 August 1939 but also gave United Kingdom residents freedom to buy gold in bar form.

Don't be lulled, however, into total complacency, thinking that completed freedom can last forever. Remember that when the French took off exchange controls they reimposed them 12 months later. A Socialist

Government returning to power in Britain could not only reimpose exchange controls (the Exchange Control Act 1947 is still on the statute books) but also clamp down on the British freedom to buy gold in coin, or bar, form for purely doctrinaire reasons.

What coins are there?

There appears to be a widespread belief that the only coins in the British market worth buying are krugerrands or sovereigns. In the USA there would be an equal belief as to the merits of double, single and half eagles; in Canada it would be the 'mapleleaf', in France it would be the 'Napoleon' and, if the Russian citizens were allowed to buy gold coins (which they aren't) in the USSR, the Chervonetz would be tops. In fact you can deal in all these coins on the London Gold Market, including the ¼ oz Chervonetz which is available from the London branch of the Moscow Narodny Bank. You really need to know just how much gold each coin contains – a piece of information resolutely witheld by The London Gold Market and by gold dealers – in order that you can work out whether or not you are paying a fair price for a coin (see Table 16).

Table 16 The gold content weight of bullion coins

Bullion gold coins	Gold content weight
King Edward sovereign (UK)	0.2354 oz
Queen Elizabeth sovereign (UK)	0.2354 oz
Krugerrand (South Africa)	1 oz
(there are also ½, ¼ and 1/10th krugerrands)	
Mapleleaf (Canada)	1 oz
Double eagle (USA)	0.9675 oz
Single eagle (USA)	0.4837 oz
Half eagle (USA)	0.2419 oz
20 franc (the 'Napoleon' – France)	0.1866 oz
100 corona (Austria)	0.9802 oz
20 lire (Italy)	0.1866 oz
50 peso (Mexico)	1.2056 oz
20 franc (Belgium)	0.1866 oz
20 mark (West Germany)	0.2054 oz
20 franc (Switzerland)	0.1866 oz
Chervonetz (USSR)	0.25 oz

In the London Gold Market coins are quoted on a 'bid' and 'offered' price basis. The lower price is the price you can sell the coins to the five members of the London Gold Market, and the higher price is the price you pay for the coins. (See Table 17 for an example of a typical spread.)

The spread is the dealer's profit; he buys at the lower price and sells at the higher price. The prices quoted on page 102 are what you would be quoted by the five members of the London Gold Market for coin purchases of ten or more, so you are talking about reasonably large scale deals, particularly on krugerrands, the mapleleaf, the Mexican 50 peso piece, or the American double eagle.

Table 17 The spread for a selection of coins for a gold price of £231 an ounce

Krugerrand	£237½ – £238¼
½ krugerrand	£122½ – £123¼
¼ krugerrand	£61¾ – £63½
1/10 krugerrand	£25¾ – £26½
Mapleleaf	£235¾ – £237¼
New Queen Elizabeth sovereign	£58¼ – £58¾
King Edward sovereign	£70 – £71
French 20 franc	£64¼ – £65¼
Mexican 50 peso	£292 – £293¼
Austrian 100 corona	£230 – £232
USA $20 double eagle	£284¾ – £286½

The five members of the London Gold Market are: Johnson, Matthey, Mocatta and Goldsmid, Samuel Montagu, N. M. Rothschild, and Sharps, Pixley. On the whole, these bullion houses, which meet for the gold fixing held twice daily at Rothschild's, deal in the wholesale gold market by means of transactions involving the 400 ounce standard gold bar. They aren't over-interested in small orders from the private investor, although one or two may be prepared to consider lower scale orders for coins. There are plenty of other coin dealers around but you have to bear in mind that, for example, South Africa uses the London Gold Market as one of its sales outlets for gold bar and gold coins, so the dealers have to buy their coins from the Gold Market and add their profit on top before selling to the public. (There is a sixth member of the London Gold Market – Derby & Co, part of Engelhard Industries – which doesn't attend the gold fixings.)

The premium

The reason why it is worth studying the intrinsic gold content of each gold coin is because it enables you to work out how much over the odds you are paying ('the premium') for buying gold in coin form as opposed to gold in bar form.

Let's go through the list (Tables 18 and 19) and you can see how to work out the premium for yourself, taking the price of gold at £231 an ounce and leaving aside VAT.

As you can see, the smaller the coin when it comes to krugerrands the higher the premium – ranging from just over 3 per cent for the full kruger down to almost 15 per cent for the one-tenth krugerrand.

Let's see how some of the other coins compare (Table 19). You can do the same thing with a pocket calculator with any of the other coins listed to find out how much over the odds you are paying for the intrinsic gold content of the coin you are buying.

In the case of the 20 franc gold 'Napoleon' – by inserting the appropriate figures in exactly the same way, we find the gold content is worth £43.10p against the gold market price of £65.25p (a difference of £22.15p or a premium of 51 per cent). In the case of the Mexican 50 peso piece the gold

Table 18 The intrinsic gold content of krugerrands

Coin	Gold market price (with gold at £231 per troy oz)	Gold content	Premium over gold price
Krugerrand	£238.25	1 oz	3.1 per cent
(Calculation: £238.25 minus £231 = £7.25 and $\frac{\pounds 7.25}{\pounds 231}$ = 3.1 per cent)			
½ krugerrand	£123.25	½ oz	6.7 per cent
(Calculation: £123.25 minus £115.50 = £7.75 and $\frac{\pounds 7.75}{\pounds 115.50}$ = 6.7 per cent)			
¼ krugerrand	£63.50	¼ oz	10 per cent
(Calculation: £63.50 minus £57.75 = £5.75 and $\frac{\pounds 5.75}{\pounds 57.75}$ = 10 per cent)			
1/10 krugerrand	£26.50	1/10 oz	14.7 per cent
(Calculation: £26.50 minus £23.10 = £3.40 and $\frac{\pounds 3.40}{\pounds 23.10}$ = 14.7 per cent)			

Table 19 The intrinsic gold content of three other coins

Coin	Gold market price	Gold content	Premium over gold price
King Edward sovereign	£71	0.2354 oz	31 per cent
(Calculation: £231 × 0.2354 = £54.38p and £71 minus £54.38 = £16.62 and $\frac{\pounds 16.62}{\pounds 54.38}$ = 31 per cent)			
Queen Elizabeth sovereign	£58.75	0.2354 oz	8 per cent
(Calculation: £231 × 0.2354 = £54.38p and £58.75 minus £54.38 = £4.37 and $\frac{\pounds 4.37}{\pounds 54.38}$ = 8 per cent)			
Double eagle	£286.50	0.9675 oz	28 per cent
(Calculation: £231 × 0.9675 = £223.49p and £286.50 minus £223.49 = £63.01 and $\frac{\pounds 63.01}{\pounds 223.49}$ = 28.1 per cent)			

content is worth £278.49p against a market price of £293.25p, throwing up a premium of 5 per cent.

As you can see there are wide differences in the premiums you pay for different coins and, I repeat, it is worth doing the calculations yourself to see how much extra you are paying for gold in coin form as against gold in bar form, assuming you could get gold in such small bars (which you can – from

Standard & Chartered Bank which we'll come to in Chapter 23). Of course, the buyer of a gold coin who pays the premium will get it back on sale to a lesser or greater extent. The important point to realise is that the premium can change. For example in the British Gold Rush of 1974 the krugerrand premium went to over 20 per cent but, if you had sold the coin in early 1981, the premium had slipped back to the 3 per cent mark. Not that you would have noticed because your capital gain on the transaction would have been big enough to drive all considerations of the fluctuation in the premium from your head, as you can see from Table 20.

Table 20 The fluctuations of the krugerrand premium

	Average price of krugerrands	Rise/fall over previous year (per cent)
January 1972	£17.50	–
January 1973	£28.20	+61.1
January 1974	£49.35	+75.0
January 1975	£75.50	+52.98
January 1976	£71.40	−5.43
January 1977	£80.25	+12.39
January 1978	£92.50	+15.26
January 1979	£118.50	+28.1
January 1980	£367.50	+210.1
January 1981	£266.00	−27.6
January 1982	£212.50	−20.1
January 1983	£338.25	+59.2

It is possible to lose money too – for example if you had bought krugers in 1975 and sold them the following year, or if you had bought them during the world-wide flight into gold following the Russian invasion of Afghanistan in January 1980 and sold them the following year when somewhat calmer conditions prevailed on the international political scene.

Capital gains tax and gold coins

Sovereigns are capital gains tax free as they are (technically) coins of the realm. This is one argument for buying sovereigns, and paying the higher premium, rather than buying krugerrands or other imported gold coins. Gains from gold coins appear to be something of a grey area so far as the Inland Revenue's policy on capital gains tax is concerned. Gains may be treated as capital gains subject to the capital gains tax charge, after deducting capital losses and taking into account your allowances before any capital gains tax comes into play. On the other hand, capital gains on gold coins can be treated as income and taxed as such, most probably at a much higher rate than the capital gains tax rate.

Whether you get lumbered with your gain being treated, for tax purposes, as income, or as capital gain, depends on your local tax inspector. The policy appears to differ between one tax office and another. The Inland

Revenue's official stance on the matter was spelled out to Deloitte, Haskins & Sells (a leading firm of accountants) in 1979. The Inland Revenue wrote: 'If the krugerrands were held for 20 years or so, the inspector will accept a claim for capital gains tax assessment.' The Inland Revenue added words to the effect that if you can demonstrate that you are not constantly dealing in krugerrands, you have a reasonable chance of assessment at capital gains tax rates. The trouble is the Inland Revenue won't define what they mean by 'constant dealing', hence the difference in approaches by different tax offices.

Gold coins instead of interest

In January 1981, Standard Chartered Bank, Britain's fifth largest bank, introduced a novel idea to appeal to investors seeking income, plus a flutter on the gold price. If you have over £1,000 to invest with Standard Chartered, instead of getting interest on your deposit, you can elect to get gold coins – either krugerrands (or mini krugerrands) or sovereigns (for those who have political objections to dealing with South Africa even on the gold coin front). You get your gold coins in advance and you get your deposit back in full at the end of the year.

Mind you, the scheme is not as generous as it sounds. The deposit you make must be sufficient to earn, in interest terms, the equivalent of the purchase price of the coin, or coins, you select. The collection of the gold coins at the outset of the deposit doesn't give you an extra profit (assuming you sell them straight away) because the interest rate is calculated in such a way as to discount the early payment of interest in the form of gold coins. For example, based on a discounted one-year interest rate of 11.7 per cent, the deposit needed for a half krugerrand and a whole krugerrand (assuming a price of £124 for the half kruger and of £242 for the whole kruger) would be £1,060 and £2,068 respectively. The scheme does, however, convert possibly highly taxed interest into nil, or much lower taxed, capital gain, but the Inland Revenue keeps a wary eye on the situation and could convert your 'capital gain' back into unearned income.

Forgeries

In recent years an increasing number of counterfeit gold coins have been circulating in Britain and, because the fakes are made from the real thing – gold – it takes an expert to spot the difference. Why, you may well ask, should forgers use real gold to make fake gold coins? The answer is to be found in the hefty premium on certain gold coins, such as the George V gold sovereigns which, on the market, carry a premium of up to 30 or 40 per cent over and above the intrinsic gold content. This means that forgers, who use high quality dies, can run off a limited issue of, say, 500 George V gold sovereigns and sell them at the market price.

Other coins favoured by forgers for circulation in Britain, according to Shaw Cavendish & Co., the bullion dealers, include all £5 and £2 pieces, 1908 and 1913 sovereigns from the Ottawa Mint, 1916 and 1917 sovereigns from the London Mint and 1913 and 1914 half sovereigns. In addition, any coins of rare dates, or high value coins, should be treated with suspicion. One of the main counterfeiting centres is the Lebanon for the very good reason that it is legal in that country to make gold coins other than Lebanese coinage. Coins are sold, perfectly legitimately, from the Lebanon to countries in Africa, Asia and Latin America. Some of the coins are then smuggled into Britain – a smuggling job which is not so difficult as it sounds because gold coins don't show up on walk-through airport security machines. Organised crime syndicates in Europe are also involved, along with the private smuggling entrepreneurs.

The best forgeries weigh the same as the real coin and look alike. According to Patrick Finn, chairman of the International Bureau for the Suppression of Counterfeit Currency, one major London merchant bank unknowingly bought a sizeable hoard of fake sovereigns. As they were worth only their scrap value in gold weight, the bank lost out to the tune of at least 20 per cent – the difference between the scrap value of gold the smelters are willing to pay and the ruling gold market price, plus the premium they had paid out on the sovereigns in the first place.

How can you tell the difference? An amateur can't but sometimes an expert can tell just from throwing a fake coin down on a table and realising it doesn't ring true. Your best safeguard is to buy coins which have only a small premium over the price of gold – such as the krugerrand – which don't offer the forgers such a big return. You aren't completely safe even with krugerrands because there are many fake krugers around.

Gold bar forgeries

There are phoney gold bars as well as phoney gold coins sitting in bank vaults round the world. Enterprising forgers have realised that the weakness of the gold bar market is that most bars and ingots are not tested after their first smelting and 'assay', at which point they are stamped with the 'fineness'. To be acceptable on the London Gold Market, the bars – ranging from 250 gramme gold bars through to one kilo bars, all the way up to the 100 ounce and 400 ounce gold bars (the latter constituting the bulk of the world's wholesale gold dealing business) – have to have a fineness of from 0.995, the minimum gold content accepted, to 0.9999, which is virtually pure gold. The gold used in the manufacture of bullion gold coins is less fine than that used for gold bars – the fineness of gold in, say, a krugerrand could be around the 0.9166 mark.

The few gold bars which are tested after their first assay are normally tested by methods which would have been familiar to the ancient Greeks. A scraping of gold is taken from the surface of the gold bar to test its fineness.

Aware of this weakness in the system, the forgers will take a gold bar, already stamped and coded, remove the top, scoop out the middle and fill the bar up with wolfram or sintered tungsten. Then they weld the top back on. The bar has the look, weight, appearance and density of the real thing and passes some of today's archaic testing methods with flying colours. The only real way to test gold is to melt the whole bar down at the refinery.

This complete melt down does happen on occasions. Gold which goes to the Indian market in 10 tola bars (a tola is an Indian unit of measurement), smuggled out in specially made belts on the dhows from Dubai, fetches a handsome premium on the Indian market, as much as 100 per cent over the prevailing world gold price. The Indian gold dealers don't mind paying the premium for the smuggled gold and they like to make an extra turn on it by adding in copper when they melt the gold down for onward sale to an unsuspecting buyer who lacks the basic know-how to test the fineness of the gold. When this gold comes back to the London market it has a distinct reddish hue and stands out like a sore thumb in a bank's gold vaults against properly assayed and accepted South African, or Russian, gold. The reddish hued bars have to be melted down and refined before they can be accepted back on the London gold market.

The American Society for Testing Materials (ASTM) did establish a standard for gold testing in 1973 but there is no world-wide standard in use. This means that once gold bars get into an inter-bank circuit where they are channelled between irreproachable dealers, forgeries are virtually undetectable. Gold bars sold to private investors can be forgeries as the private investor seldom has the means to test his purchase. So be careful if gold bars or gold coins take your fancy – all that glisters *may not* be gold!

Coin mints

In the days of the Empire when the map of the world was stained liberally with Imperial red, the Royal Mint set up branches overseas. This means that not all the sovereigns of the older variety come from the Royal Mint in Britain. They emanated from Australia, from the Sydney, Perth and Melbourne Mints; from Canada, from the Ottawa Mint; from South Africa, from the Pretoria Mint and from the Indian Mint. How can you tell which mint your coin comes from? The place where a coin was minted is indicated by letters on the back of the coins, as follows:

I – Indian Mint	P – Perth Mint
SA – Pretoria Mint	S – Sydney Mint
C – Ottawa Mint	M – Melbourne Mint

From fleur de coin *to 'fine' – watch out for condition*

The condition of a coin, or how it is graded by the market, is important in the bullion gold coin world and, even more so, in the numismatic, or collectors' coin market. The slightest change in the condition of a coin or its 'patina', or the presence of any abrasions, can knock down its market value. Coins are graded as follows:

FDC – *Fleur de coin.* A coin which is in mint state and is therefore unused, flawless, without any wear, scratches or marks.

BU – Brilliant, uncirculated. This is a coin in pristine condition – as good a state as when it left the mint.

Unc – Uncirculated. A new coin issued by the Royal Mint but not necessarily perfect.

EF – Extremely fine. Close inspection may show slight surface marks, but little sign of having been in circulation.

VF – Very fine. The coin has no dents on its edge. Some wear on the high points of the design is permissible, but the coin should have no scratches on the 'field' round the design.

F – Fine. Considerable signs of wear on the raised surfaces. The lowest acceptable grade unless the coin is very rare or extremely old.

It is possible to get combinations of gradings, but only two at a time. 'VF-EF' denotes a coin whose general condition is between 'Very fine' and 'Extremely fine'; 'F/VF' means that the other side of the coin (the obverse) is in 'Fine' condition, while the other side (the reverse) is 'Very fine'. It is all too easy for the amateur to end up paying a 'Very fine' price for only a 'Fine' coin or one of even lower value.

One way to avoid being taken for a ride is to buy only from a reputable dealer who is a member of either the International Association of Professional Numismatists or the British Numismatic Trade Association, or a dealer who can offer an unconditional guarantee that the coin, or coins, you are buying from him is genuinely (and accurately) graded.

VAT and gold coins

Until 1982 gold coins didn't attract VAT (Value Added Tax) in the United Kingdom, being theoretically legal tender in the country of origin, while the gold bar did, and still does, attract VAT. Unlike most EEC countries, the United Kingdom did not charge VAT on gold coins and gold black market dealers were quick to see the profit opportunity from melting down gold coins and selling the result in bar form, plus VAT, to bullion refiners and jewellers. One enterprising crook was caught out at this game because the local electricity board in his area noticed a sharp rise in his electricity bill – caused because he had converted his front room into a gold melting furnace!

The arithmetic of such crooked dealings was simple enough – gold coins, such as the krugerrand and the Canadian mapleleaf, often sell at a premium of only around 3 per cent above the market gold price prevailing. When the VAT-free coins were converted into gold ingots, which fetched an extra 15 per cent once VAT was added on to the bill, the crooks cleared a risk-free profit of around 12 per cent – or about £25 per ounce of gold at the time. The crooks didn't send the VAT into the Customs & Excise; they pocketed their profits and disappeared. 'You could change your address, give a funny name or re-emerge as a new company later. It was just the cost of a new letterhead,' commented one leading gold dealer at the time. In early 1982, VAT was imposed on all bullion gold coins sold by dealers in the United Kingdom to eliminate the fraud, however, the fact that gold coins were sold VAT-free in the Channel Islands did produce a similar fraudulent reaction, with VAT-free coins being imported in car boots from the Channel Islands to the United Kingdom and melted down into ingots or sold on with VAT added.

The best 'melt down' coin is the Canadian mapleleaf which is made of 99.9 per cent gold which means that it can be converted easily into bars above the standard gold purity accepted on the London Gold Market of 99.5 per cent. Krugerrands, on the other hand, have enough alloy in them to reduce the gold purity to 91.6 per cent and are therefore unsuitable for melt down.

23

Operating a gold trading account

Just as you can deal in such metals as tin or copper, via a commodity broker specialising in metals or a ring dealing member of the London Metal Exchange, you can deal in gold, via a metal account.

Metal account holders have two broad options open to them – whether to hold their gold on an 'allocated' or 'unallocated' basis. Under the 'allocated' system investors have a direct claim on a specific amount of gold held in their name at their bank or by their broker. 'Unallocated' holders simply own a paper claim on the general pool of gold in the possession of the bullion broker or bank.

In either case, whether he is running an allocated or unallocated account, the investor can buy or sell gold without getting involved with physical delivery. The difference is that, in the case of an allocated account, the gold is earmarked in the bank's, or broker's, vaults ready for immediate delivery if the client so requires. The unallocated account holder has, in theory at least, less protection because if all unallocated gold account holders were to call for their gold at once, in the face of some impending world catastrophe, some wouldn't get it (assuming the catastrophe still allowed gold deliveries to take place at all) because there wouldn't be enough gold in the unallocated pool to go round.

This is because banks and dealers in unallocated gold operate rather like banks. The latter keep only a small proportion of their deposits in the form of cash, or near cash, because they don't expect every account holder to withdraw his, or her, deposit at exactly the same time although, in the old, unregulated days of the private banks in the English shires, a 'run on the bank' was not infrequent and usually resulted in its collapse. This isn't to say that dealers in unallocated gold accounts are wheeling and dealing in gold which doesn't exist at all. The gold owned by unallocated holders certainly exists, but it might be stored in a place where the investor isn't resident, for example, a UK investor would be sensible to operate an unallocated gold account via Zürich because unallocated gold is free of the 5.6 per cent purchase tax which investors are charged when taking physical delivery of gold. This is a useful saving because, in the United Kingdom, VAT is charged on all gold bar purchases, including bars in an unallocated gold account.

The flat fees charged to investors operating allocated accounts are higher than those charged on unallocated accounts because of the greater security offered to the allocated gold account holder and because keeping allocated gold is more costly for the bank or broker concerned. The difference in fees charged is not a major influence in that the banks and brokers catering for those operating gold accounts tend to deal with companies or wealthy individuals of undoubted credit standing. The majority of wealthy private investors tend to opt for the safety of the allocated gold account and pay the premium on the fees charged for the extra protection and security.

The Swiss banks thought, until the sales tax was placed on gold, that Zürich was the favourite haven for gold account holders in the Middle East, channelling part of their petrodollar fortunes into gold in Zürich as insurance against possible palace coups. Once the Swiss did impose their sales tax, some of the Arab account holders switched to London. However, the ultra-cautious know that Switzerland, or United Kingdom, is not that far away from the Russian tanks if the worst came to the worst, and suspect that the Russians wouldn't make an elaborate deviation around Switzerland to ensure continued Swiss neutrality if the Third World War were to break out. Therefore some people prefer to keep their gold in the last bastion of capitalism, the USA, which also has the military might to oppose the USSR (or alternatively in Canada which is well under the US umbrella). It is the same thinking which causes Arabs with petrodollars to spare to invest in large tracts of the Middle West, despite the low income yield offered by farm land – they know it can't run away and hopefully they'll be around to take possession of their investment when the time is right.

Unless you have over $250,000 to spare for speculation in gold, your custom won't be of interest to the five members which make up the London Gold Market, although one of the five – Johnson, Matthey – may be prepared to deal for smaller amounts.

The gold fixing meeting takes place twice each working day at the offices of Rothschild's. Rather like a stately war-game, the five representatives of the five bullion houses (N. M. Rothschild, Mocatta and Goldsmid, Johnson, Matthey, Samuel Montagu and Sharps, Pixley) have little flags with which to signal their intentions to the other participants. Each representative is in direct contact with his own gold-dealing desk. In turn, the dealers at the gold desks are in contact with their clients who may be millionaires living in tax exile in Switzerland, large companies dealing in gold, banks, or wealthy Arabs placing some of their vast petrodollar revenues into gold. Some of the clients will be buyers; some will be sellers.

At the morning and afternoon 'fixings', economists would say the conditions for a 'perfect market' are being achieved. At various gold price levels the buyers and sellers will be out of balance until a price is arrived at at which the supply of gold from the sellers will be balanced by the buying of gold by the purchasers. At this point the price of gold is 'fixed'. Once the price is fixed, the dealers at each bullion house get to work on their telephones, signalling the London fixing price throughout the international gold market. It's a scene of frenetic activity for the half hour, or so, following the gold price fixing. (Woe betide anyone who unknowingly rings up a gold dealer during the fixing, or in the half hour afterwards, with some unimportant question.)

At one time the London fixing governed the price of gold world wide, providing a benchmark for trading until the next fixing. Now its importance has diminished as other gold markets have grown in prominence. The Hong Kong Gold Market has the advantage of being the first to open (eight hours ahead of London) and can often set the pace for the rest of the gold markets during the ensuing day, particularly during a period of volatility on the gold price front.

Each of the bullion houses has vaults with gold storage facilities. In fact the vaults are so ultra-safe and the security systems so sophisticated that a mouse scampering across the floor has been enough to alert the monitor system – run from the control room of a security firm – and result in the key holder being brought from his warm bed to the bank's premises. This enables the police to check whether anything is going on although, in the inner sanctum of the gold vaults, the main gold safe into which one can walk has a vast steel door which, once opened, will normally be governed by a time lock. Across the floor and area of the anteroom to the main gold safe the electronic sensors lurk ready for the unwary, as do the pressure pads and closed circuit television scanners roaming across the vaults.

Any visitor to a bullion house vaults will see stacks of the standard 400 ounce gold bars along with the smaller ingots – the one kilo, the 10 tola – the pyramids of gold grain and the rather ugly breeze blocks which are silver in its unpolished state. Gold bars certainly live up to their name. Even in the gloom of the vaults they provide a glow as if from some inner source of light. The account-holders with the bullion houses may rarely, if ever, see the gold they own. Deals conducted at the London gold fixing will mean that one, two, or even ten, standard gold bars will be moved from one stack to another in the same vault – thus indicating a change of ownership. On the other hand, some prefer to have gold in their own possesion – either transferred to a bank vault in Switzerland or moved to a bank vault in a tax haven such as Jersey (there is no VAT in Jersey and VAT on a standard gold bar can be a substantial sum if physical delivery is taken in London, or when sales tax is charged in Switzerland, West Germany or the USA).

While the bullion houses may deal with the exotic world of the jet set they are all firmly within the British banking system. Samuel Montagu, for instance, is a wholly owned subsidiary of Midland Bank. Sharps, Pixley is owned by merchant bankers Kleinwort Benson; Mocatta and Goldsmid is owned by Standard and Chartered Bank. As the bullion houses operate in a highly volatile market, they tend to err on the cautious side insofar as gold is concerned. Mocatta, for example, balances its bullion-dealing books at the end of each trading day and also places strict limits on risk exposure throughout the day.

You can, of course, deal in other gold markets – and many of the big investors do so. For example the Luxembourg Stock Exchange holds a gold fixing daily at 10.30 am local time. This market has been promoted by five banks – Banque Internationale de Luxembourg, Banque Nationale de Paris, Caisse d'Epargne de l'Etat, Dresdner Bank International and Kredietbank SA Luxembourgeoise. Backing them up are some 20 members of the Luxembourg Stock Exchange operating as market makers. One advantage of dealing through Luxembourg (in addition to keeping one's gold dealing affairs away from the scrutiny of the United Kingdom Inland Revenue) is that there is no VAT or sales tax to worry about.

The Zürich market in Switzerland emerged as the world's leading gold market, particularly when the Soviet Union channelled its main sales through Zürich to the western world. You can easily tell that Zürich is a gold trading centre – gold beckons the prospective investor from many a bank and shop window in the city's Bahnhofstrasse, reminding him that he should store part of his wealth in this tried and trusted metal.

As long as the gold price was controlled by the Western central banks, London was the undisputed centre of the world gold market. Zürich came to the fore in 1968 with the re-emergence of a free market in gold, running in tandem with the official market. The Zürich Market itself stems from the Zürich Gold Pool formed in 1968 by the 'Big Three' Swiss banks – the Swiss Bank Corporation, the Union Bank and the Swiss Credit Bank. By adopting a united front they were able to swing the South African gold output towards Zürich. South Africa, in addition to the commercial inducements offered, was also disenchanted with the attitude of the United Kingdom to apartheid and proceeded to award Zürich with nearly all its output.

Today, the Swiss gold market consists of the 'Big Three' plus the Bank Leu and the Trade Development Bank in Geneva. Only the 'Big Three' are members of the gold pool. No gold, by the way, accumulates in the 'pool' for any length of time. It is merely a mechanism for clearing gold-dealing operations between the three banks (which act in concert) and holds their prices in line. It is Zürich's answer to the London 'gold fixing'. The difference is that the Zürich pool price is a market price with a spread between bid and offer, whose significance for the prospective buyer or seller is that it is backed by the biggest collective dealer in the gold business. While the London market tends to pursue the role of a broker, matching supply and demand, the Zürich banks act as dealers and also take sizeable positions themselves.

Gold buying from abroad can be arranged by mail and the Swiss bank concerned will store an overseas customer's gold in a safe-keeping account, costing around Sw. F.1.25 per Sw. F.1,000 worth of gold (with a minimum charge of Sw. F.10). Alternatively, the investor can buy gold via a claim account which entitles him to gold without physically allocating any to him. The cost is slightly smaller – 0.1 per cent yearly on the credit balance.

All three major Swiss banks have their own gold refineries: Metaux Precieux (Swiss Bank Corporation), Valcambi (Credit Suisse) and Argor (Union Bank). These turn out an impressive range of small bars ranging from 5 gm to 12½ kg. For the coin bug, Bank Leu specialises in this particular market, being the leading Swiss dealer in gold coins, particularly numismatic, or collector's, coins.

Today Zürich still handles the greater part of South African gold – around three-quarters – and, since 1972, Russia has added to Zürich's throughput, selling a large part of its variable annual sale to the Swiss banks via the Zürich-based Wozchod Handelsbank. The net result is that over half of the new gold flowing on to the markets of the free world is now sold through Zürich.

Whereas London remains pre-eminent as a clearing centre for international gold transactions, Zürich is probably the place where the greatest physical movement of gold takes place, vividly illustrated by Table 21 which, albeit, only shows the flow of gold coming to Zürich from the Middle and Far East

Table 21 The Eastern gold trail

Net physical movements to and from European bullion centres (tonnes)	1979	1980	swing
Singapore – London*	−39	+31	+ 70
Singapore – Zürich*	−22	− 3	+ 19
Hong Kong – London†	−63	− 2	+ 61
Hong Kong – Zürich	−26	− 5	+ 21
Beirut – Zürich	−53	+80	+133
(+/− denotes flow into/out of Europe)			

* First 6 months of 1980
† First 11 months of 1980
(Sources: Singapore, Hong Kong, Swiss trade statistics)

West German wealth, the traditional French love affair with gold and the Italian interest in a politically secure investment are all on Switzerland's doorstep. And within Switzerland the country's watch and jewellery industry takes up a good volume of gold, on top of international demand.

The world of the metal brokers

If the amount of cash you have to devote to gold speculation is not enough to catch the interest of the bullion houses running the gold market, but is enough (£5,000 plus) to attract the services of a broker, you can deal with one of the members of the London Metal Exchange – Fig. 8 shows the ring-dealing membership and where they sit, while Table 22 gives you an at-a-glance guide to the market hours during which all metals are dealt with:

Table 22 London Metal Exchange market hours

Morning market		Afternoon market	
Options (in all metals)	11.45 to 11.50 a.m.	Lead/Zinc	3.30 to 3.45 p.m.
Silver	11.50 to 11.55 a.m.	Copper wirebars/Cathodes	3.35 to 3.40 p.m.
Aluminium	11.55 to 12.00 noon	Tin	3.40 to 3.45 p.m.
Copper	12.00 to 12.05 p.m.	Aluminium/Nickel	3.45 to 3.50 p.m.
Tin	12.05 to 12.10 p.m.	Silver	3.50 to 3.55 p.m.
Lead	12.10 to 12.15 p.m.	Interval	3.55 to 4.00 p.m.
Zinc	12.15 to 12.20 p.m.	Lead	4.00 to 4.05 p.m.
Nickel	12.20 to 12.25 p.m.	Zinc	4.05 to 4.10 p.m.
Interval	12.25 to 12.30 p.m.	Copper wirebars	4.10 to 4.15 p.m.
Copper wirebars	12.30 to 12.35 p.m.	Copper cathodes	4.15 to 4.20 p.m.
Copper cathodes & Fire refined	12.35 to 12.40 p.m.	Tin	4.20 to 4.25 p.m.
		Aluminium	4.25 to 4.30 p.m.
Tin	12.40 to 12.45 p.m.	Nickel	4.30 to 4.35 p.m.
Lead	12.45 to 12.50 p.m.	Silver	4.35 to 4.40 p.m.
Zinc	12.50 to 12.55 p.m.	Kerb trading until	4.55 p.m.
Aluminium	12.55 to 1.00 p.m.		
Nickel	1.00 to 1.05 p.m.		
Silver	1.05 to 1.10 p.m.		
Kerb trading until	1.25 p.m.		

Note: The second morning session, which commences at 12.30 p.m., is the official Ring of the day when the prices, reached during the five minutes of trading, are monitored by the Quotations Committee. These prices are read out at 1.10 p.m. by the Secretary and constitute the official prices of the day.

Dealers sit in a ring, each seat being assigned to a company. Behind each seat is a telephone booth enabling dealers to keep in direct contact with their offices and clients. The ring itself is backed up by communications services, offices and other facilities.

Together with its infrastructure, the ring is housed in Plantation House in Fenchurch Street and in Mincing Lane. Despite its modest frontage the London Metal Exchange can accommodate 5,000 people. Previously the Exchange was based for 98 years in Whittington Avenue near Leadenhall Market, on the site of the Roman Forum, and before that it was in Lombard Court.

A visitor to the modern Metal Exchange, which was opened in 1980, will see two main areas – a double height area of 325 square metres and 200 square metres of single storey adjoining area. In the double height space, top lit by a skylight which allows some natural light, the visitor's gaze naturally focusses on the main dealing ring. This is a fixed circle of red leather seats capable of providing room for 36 member companies.

Four columns mark the entry points to the ring. Each seat in the ring corresponds to a communications booth which carries the same number.

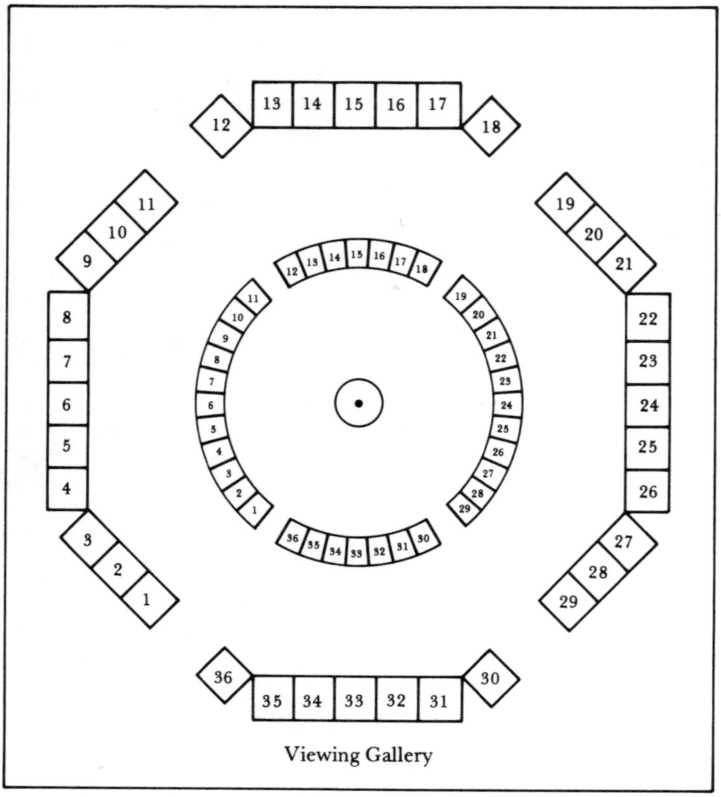

KEY to the booth numbers and members of the new London Metal Exchange at Plantation House in Fenchurch Street:

1. Empty.
2. Tennant Trading (Metals) Ltd.
3. Phillip and Lion.
4. Lonconex Ltd.
5. The Commercial Metal Co. Ltd.
6. Empty.
7. Cerro Metals (UK) Ltd.
8. J. H. Rayner (Mincing Lane) Ltd.
9. Ametalco Trading Ltd.
10. Billiton-Enthoven Metals Ltd.
11. Empty.
12. Brandeis, Goldschmidt & Co. Ltd.
13. Metdist Ltd.
14. Triland Metals Ltd.
15. Sogemin (Metals) Ltd.
16. Intsel Ltd.
17. Maclaine, Watson & Co. Ltd.
18. Associated Lead Manufacturers Ltd.
19. Amalgamated Metal Trading Ltd.
20. Holco Trading Co.
21. Cominco (UK) Ltd.
22. Continental Ore Europe Ltd.
23. Gerald Metals Ltd.
24. Rostrum (Adjacent).
25. Henry Bath & Son Ltd.
26. Anglo Chemical Metals Ltd.
27. Johnson Matthey Bankers Ltd.
28. Rudolf Wolff & Co. Ltd.
29. Leopold Lazarus Ltd.
30. Gill & Duffus Ltd.
31. Metallgesellschaft Limited.
32. Boustead Davis (Metal Brokers) Ltd.
33. Wilson, Smithett & Cope Ltd.
34. Sharps, Pixley Ltd.
35. Entores (Metal Brokers) Ltd.
36. Empty.

Flashing lights on the back of the seat indicate to the dealer that his telephones are ringing in his booth. Each booth has 12 telephone lines as well as small television screens for visual data display which are linked to a central indicator system.

At the sharp end

The London Metal Exchange ring members are at the sharp end of the business, operating in a frenetic environment in volatile markets which can be affected by all sorts of unpredictable events, from a fear of a boost in interest rates to a Russian invasion of Afghanistan. They are operating to make profits for their clientele who may be large companies needing metals (including gold) for their manufacturing processes, or clients speculating on metals (including gold) for commodity funds based offshore, for in-house, unofficial syndicates of small investors pooling their funds, and for their own firms. The rewards for successful anticipation of market trends can be very high indeed – but the penalties for the reverse are just as high.

For the private client, the highest risk, and highest reward, strategy is to open an account with a metal broker dealing on the gold futures market. Even then, he has two choices open to him. He can hand his cash over to be managed by an expert – the so called 'discretionary account'. This has the advantage that you don't have to make buying and selling decisions yourself, so you are relieved of that responsibility. Discretionary accounts are less risky also because, as the commodity broker makes the dealing decisions for you and will not want to lose a client, he will probably pursue a fairly conservative investment policy on your behalf. The other advantage is that you have 'limited liability' in the sense that you cannot lose more than the original amount of the capital you hand over. The broker sends in his monthly statement of your account, and you will be charged his brokerage commission – so it's worth ringing round a few brokers to ask for a list of their brokerage charges.

The alternative choice is the more risky 'trading account'. This means you monitor the gold – or any other metal – price yourself, make your own decisions when to buy and sell, and the broker collects a straightforward brokerage charge. When you complete a client's agreement form for a trading account, the broker will check out your credit standing. This is because you can take advantage of the gearing leverage available on the commodities futures market, including the gold futures market. However, you have to be prepared to make available additional cash so that you can top up your margins if the market goes against you. The doctrine of unlimited liability prevails in direct dealing of this type, and you, the client,

◁ Fig. 8 The London Metal Exchange ring dealing members. (This list was correct at the time of going to press.)

bear all the risks, plus indemnifying the broker in the event of default on your account.

Using a strategy

In gold speculation via a broker the first thing to watch out for is a major price trend. The problem is that it is difficult to spot when a trend is at the beginning, middle, or end of its course. If you can establish your position in the direction of a major trend and you can keep that position through one-third of the movement, then you should reap good profits. But risk only a small amount of your trading capital in any one deal. You can't afford to have a position counter to a major trend and to hold it for any length of time because you would absorb all your trading capital. So cut your losses and let your profits run.

Use stop orders to limit your exposure to a big loss. A stop order becomes a market order when the stop price, which can be fixed above or below the market price at which you buy, is reached.

Gold options trading started on the London Gold Futures Market in 1983. The great attraction of options is that they provide a means of trading in futures with a known maximum loss – the premium paid if the option to buy or sell at a specified date is not exercised.

About taxation

The Inland Revenue's treatment of gains from gold speculation is something of a grey area (in fact, the taxation map has more grey-shaded areas than black or white ones). There are no firm rulings on whether gains should be liable to capital gains tax or to the bigger burden of income tax. Decisions vary between tax districts and also between individual cases. In practice, commodity brokers have found that buyers of physical commodities frequently manage to get gains assessed under capital gains tax. Capital gains on gold futures are more likely to be taxed as income, particularly if the speculative nature of the operation is reinforced by borrowings with which to finance the deals. Funds placed under professional management (offshore commodity trusts) can be categorised usually as capital gains if capital gains are, in fact, made, and so they are taxed as such.

24

Using the gold futures market

The Americans treat gold just like any other commodity. And just like any other commodity you can operate on the futures market in the US, the Far East, or in the London Gold Futures Market. The big advantage to the out and out speculator is that the existence of a futures market enables him to 'gear up', so that a limited amount of money (which can be his own cash, or money borrowed from a bank) can be used to 'take a position' over a much larger value of gold. This means the prospective gains can be multiplied seven, or even ten, times, depending on how much you are called on to put down at the outset. The other advantage of gold futures contracts is that the buyer need never take physical delivery of the gold, although he can do so if he wants. In this way he is able to wheel and deal in gold without running into the problems of paying VAT if he takes delivery of gold in Britain, or paying a sales tax if he takes delivery in the USA, Switzerland or West Germany, and he has no transport, insurance, or storage costs to take into account. The bulk – 90 per cent or more – of gold futures contracts is liquidated before they reach maturity.

The London gold futures market

For British – or West European – residents, the London gold futures markets offer easier access than the gold futures markets in the USA or in the Far East. Launched in 1982, the London market was unique in that it was the only one to offer a sterling contract for gold futures contracts, as opposed to the US dollar contract. This proved so unpopular that it was replaced with a US dollar contract soon after. Trading is carried out on a monthly basis with deliveries, in London, due at the end of the trading month – unlike the London Metal Exchange where contracts are for same day settlement so many months in advance.

While the new gold futures market originally set its sights to attract a wider range of clients (both investors and companies using gold in jewellery, in electronic circuitry or in dentistry), the minimum amount in which an investor is able to deal is 100 ounces because each futures contract is for 100 ounces. Even at the one contract level, the investor with undoubted credit standing and plenty of cash available for topping up his margin requirements (in case the gold price goes against him) if called upon so to do, would have to part with £3,360 by way of deposit on a futures contract. This is assuming that the deposit is set at 15 per cent, which would give the investor a gearing up factor of 7. An initial deposit call of 10 per cent would give a gearing up factor of 10. That £3,360 deposit, by the way, assumes a gold price of £224 an ounce (£224 times 100 ounces times 15 per cent).

Dealings in the market are cleared and underwritten by the International Commodities Clearing House. There is a separate operation running the market which is called the London Gold Futures Market and this is 50 per cent owned by the London Gold Market Ltd (the bullion dealers who run the wholesale London Gold Market) and 50 per cent owned by the London Metal Exchange's holding company, the London Metal Market and Exchange Ltd.

At this stage you are well entitled to ask for an explanation of exactly what a gold futures contract is, and how the speculator can make a killing from its use. A gold futures contract is a piece of paper which binds you to buy or sell a quantity of gold at a precise time in the future at a price agreed at the time the contract is taken out. The contract also details the standards the gold has to meet in order to be acceptable for delivery.

To enter into a futures contract a buyer or seller is asked by his gold broker – whether in London, Chicago or one of the Far Eastern markets – to provide a deposit, or margin, which can be 10 per cent or 15 per cent (or even 50 per cent) of the contract's value. This is where the speculator's ability to make his killing comes from because he gains gearing or, in US parlance, 'leverage' – he gets the ability to control large amounts of gold for a relatively small outlay.

Fortunes have been made and lost by speculative gambling on gold using gearing up opportunities. Anyone who borrowed to the limit, and over it, back in the autumn of 1979, and used his borrowings to take a position over ten times the value of his deposit, could have made himself a millionaire had he had the good sense, when gold was streaking up to the $850 an ounce mark in January 1980, after the Russian invasion of Afghanistan, to sell out, repay his borrowings and go and live in a sun-soaked villa in the South of France. The reverse side of the picture is that many a speculator buying in on borrowed money, and dealing on the margin, when the gold price passed through the $700 an ounce mark, could have been (and many were) wiped out when the gold price crashed back to under the $400 an ounce mark. When the timing is wrong and the speculator loses all, the human side of the tragedy tends to appear in the form of an advertisement for a house – 'must sell at any price' – on the information boards at the commodity markets.

Brokers act as the middlemen, for a negotiable brokerage fee, in all gold futures trading, whether on the London Gold Futures Market or the gold futures market run as part of the International Monetary Market of the Chicago Mercantile Exchange. Once you take a position on the gold futures market, either by buying, or selling, one or more gold futures contracts, you have two options. Either you maintain your position until the contract matures and then accept, or deliver, the gold contracted for. Alternatively you offset the contract before maturity by taking a position equal and opposite to the original trade. For example if you originally bought one gold contract, you could liquidate or offset by selling that contract.

Your offsetting deal has to be made for the same delivery month and on the same exchange as the original contract was taken out. Well over 90 per cent of all gold futures contracts are liquidated before maturity. As a result there is an enormous pyramid of paper poised on its apex on a relatively small foundation of gold. Chaos would be caused on the world gold markets if every gold futures contract holder decided to opt for physical delivery. Enough chaos was caused back in the mid 1970s when the Hunt brothers disrupted the world silver market by insisting on physical delivery in their first attempt to corner the world silver market.

While there is tremendous speculative activity on the gold futures market, sight should not be lost of the fact that the primary purpose of the market is to offer those companies which need gold for processing, for jewellery, or for electronics, an opportunity to hedge against future price fluctuations. 'Hedgers' use the futures market – just as they do any forward market whether in commodities or in financial instruments – to provide themselves with certainty, so they know at the outset exactly what their profit will be on a deal. (Look at the case of a jeweller's use of the futures market outlined in Table 23.)

Table 23 A jeweller's use of the futures market

Cash gold market	Time	Futures market
Jeweller orders gold for delivery in early April knowing the maximum price he can pay to make a profit on gold jewellery is £225 an ounce.	September	Buys April gold futures at £210 an ounce.
Buys cash gold at £250 an ounce.	April	Sells April gold futures at £245 an ounce.

The £35 an ounce profit in the futures transaction more than offsets the increase on the cash gold market from £225 to £250, so the jeweller can start work in September, knowing exactly where he stands on his raw material costs and his eventual profit at the end of the day – and picks up an additional profit on the futures market.

The New York Gold Futures Market is constantly reporting record turnovers, followed by the Chicago Mercantile Exchange which has a very similar contract. This enables some heavy arbitrage (taking advantage of price differentials in different markets) to take place between New York, Chicago and London and the Far Eastern markets.

US commodity funds

Just as in the United Kingdom (where the commodity funds are normally based in the offshore islands, the favourite being Jersey) the United States offers the investor a range of commodity funds which are less risky than operating an account via a broker. Most of the commodity funds offered by the brokerage houses in the US (most are registered with the US Securities and Exchange Commission, although a number of offshore funds are not registered) involve four parties. There is the investor, or 'limited partner' whose liability is limited to the amount originally invested – typically units are valued at $1,000 with a minimum investment of five units, or $5,000. Funds are usually closed to new investors after an initial offer period. Then there is the general partner who tends to be an affiliate or subsidiary of a broker who sponsors the funds. There is also the sponsoring brokerage firm through which all trading is done. Finally there is the investment manager who makes all the crucial decisions. The rewards of the management are high – the management fee being anything between 3 per cent and 6 per cent of the funds' assets each quarter, plus an incentive fee ranging from 10 to 15 per cent of the profits (if any). Typically around 5 per cent of an investor's original outlay goes to the sponsoring broker.

The Far East

Both Hong Kong and Singapore have gold futures markets. Until its establishment in Hong Kong, the gold dealing community had three other gold markets to cater for them. The first is the old Chinese Gold and Silver Exchange Society (Kam Ngan) dealing in physical gold only – no silver – and still operating on archaic units of taels rather than ounces (one tael equals 1.2 fine ounces). The second is the 'loco' London Market which carries on business on the basis of the London Gold Market but during Hong Kong trading hours. (Hong Kong is eight hours ahead of GMT and can set world gold prices.) The third Hong Kong market is the 'Local Comex' (New York Commodities Exchange) which is an out-of-hours Comex-based informal market made by some of the big commodity trading houses. The Hong Kong Commodities Exchange gold futures market is modelled on that of Comex although delivery is in London rather than New York, and the contract size is 100 ounces.

Singapore had opened its gold futures market prior to that of Hong Kong and, in order to keep business flowing to its market, the Singapore Gold Exchange has offered investors inducements such as the introduction of a kilobar contract along with the standard 100 ounce contract. Since the Chinese indicated their possessive interest in Hong Kong, Singapore has grown in popularity.

The USA

Since the complete relaxation of exchange controls on British residents in October 1979, the British have been free to deal in any market in the world and on any futures market – which includes the gold futures market of both Chicago and New York. The difficulties of so doing are the differences in time between the United Kingdom and the USA and the differences in practices – although there are plenty of American commodity broking operations with London offices who will handle large orders from customers wishing to wheel and deal on the Chicago or New York gold futures market or on any commodity future ranging from pork bellies to soya beans. Futures trading is the front line of the capitalist ethos.

To the outsider viewing the US markets during trading hours, especially at the opening each morning, a scene from Dante's *Inferno* opens up before his bewildered gaze. The crescendo of noise is frightening as traders in the pits shout, scream, push, grab and sometimes even punch their fellow traders in the frantic pursuit of the goddess of wealth. In spite of this, the markets are the most efficient in the world. Prices conceived in the maelstrom of the pits are flashed up on the boards within seconds and are sent round the world in under a minute as the communications network takes over. Slips of paper casually thrown down by traders in the pits are gathered up by armies of young messengers, carefully checked and then put into the system under which fortunes are made and lost daily.

Instead of buying gold, or speculating on gold futures, you can hedge your bets by buying bonds or certificates linked to the price of gold, or you can even bet on the yellow metal via the IG Index. Therefore you can play the gold market without having to worry about storage and insurance costs and without the sleepless nights which the highly volatile gold futures market could bring you.

The French gold bonds

Take the French gold bonds, for example. The Pinay bond – so called after the French Finance Minister who introduced it – has had a rocket-like ascent since the early months of 1979 following a slower,but steadier, climb in the five years before. Together with the Giscard gold-linked bond it is one of the most heavily traded investment sectors in France.

The Pinay (more correctly called the 4½ per cent French State 2007 bond) has a small interest rate of 4½ per cent of its par value which was originally Fr. F.100 – the minimum amount you could buy. The reason for its tremendous popularity is that its redemption price is linked directly to that most beloved of French coins, the 20 franc gold 'Napoleon'. The French place great faith in this coin after their experiences with paper currency and paper investments in a century which has included two world wars, German occupations, and periodic bouts of rip-roaring inflation. In fact, because of its popularity, the gold Napoleon normally stands at a hefty premium over the same amount of gold in bar form, which the French can also buy. The Napoleon-linked Pinay bond has decided advantages for the French. For a start it can be bought 'on the margin' (20 per cent down) in the market and it can be bought for relatively small sums, whereas the one kilo bar of gold commands a hefty price. Best of all it is reasonably certain that the Government will honour the redemption terms because the bond is redeemed continually by means of a sinking fund.

The 7 per cent 1988 Giscard bond is different. Its par value of Fr. F.1,000 makes it a substantial purchase for the small investor seeking a flutter on the gold market via a gold bond. Unlike the Pinay bond, the redemption terms of the Giscard bond are linked in a fairly complicated fashion to the price of gold. At times the market price of the bond has stood at a discount to its gold value to the tune of over 40 per cent. The main reason for this is a lurking suspicion among the French that the French Government will not honour the gold-linked redemption price in 1988. The cost of doing so in a single year would be astronomic, hence the lurking doubts. Also, the Government has been known to change the rules while the game is still being played, as proved by the case of the Caisse Nationale de L'Energie bond. The interest and redemption values of this were based on the revenues of the French electricity and gas corporations.

The peculiarity of the Giscard bond is the fall-back clause which ties its interest and capital repayments to the price of gold ingots in certain situations. This guarantee was to come into play if the link between gold and Western currencies was abandoned during the lifetime of the bond. At a time when the French gilt-edged market needed a boost, Giscard d'Estaing, then the high-flying Finance Minister, calculated that a bond promising the investor a type of 'paper gold' had the right marketing appeal.

Sod's law came into play when the International Monetary Fund, meeting in Jamaica in 1976, abandoned the monetary link between world currencies and gold, and France's commitments on the Giscard bond started to spiral. As a result the interest payments on the bonds in 1979 and 1980 amounted exactly to the total cash raised by the Government in the first place – Fr. F.6.5 billion – and estimates of future interest payments over the life of the bond are set at Fr. F.37 billion. Capital repayments on maturity could reach Fr. F.60 billion – ten times the original amount of funds raised, quite apart from the massive interest burden.

Gold-linked certificates

If you prefer to deal with an English speaking country, at least two US banks offer gold-linked certificates, of which the best known is the giant Citibank. The latter has its United Kingdom headquarters in the Strand. It doesn't offer a gold-linked certificate facility to United Kingdom residents from its London office, but you can deal direct with the US operation (Citibank NA, Precious Metals, 399 Park Avenue, New York, New York 10043, USA).

In banker's parlance a Citibank Gold Certificate is a 'non-negotiable depositary receipt', which, translated, means you buy a piece of paper showing that you own a specific amount of gold. The 'non-negotiable' reference means you can't sell that piece of paper in a secondary market in the way that you can sell, say, local authority negotiable bonds. Citibank backs each certificate with full 100 per cent holdings of gold. It buys the gold on your behalf, stores it and, if you want to take physical delivery of the gold, Citibank will arrange this for you in Delaware, London or Zürich.

The smallest amount of gold you can buy is $1,000, after this minimum stake, you can buy in multiples of $100. Citibank charges a commission of 3 per cent on the purchase if you buy up to $50,000 worth. A 2 per cent commission is charged if you buy between $50,000 and $100,000 worth and, once you top the $100,000 mark, the commission drops to 1¾ per cent. In addition Citibank charges a holding fee while storing your gold of ½ per cent of the value of your gold holding, but there is no charge made in the calendar year of purchase, which is to the advantage of the in and out operators. When you sell your gold, or have it delivered to you, Citibank charges a fee of 1 per cent of the value of your gold at the prevailing market price.

What the Citibank Gold Certificate offers is flexibility because it gives you several redemption options which can be exercised at any time. You can sell all, or only a portion of, the gold represented by your certificate, or you can take physical delivery. So far as VAT or sales tax is concerned, there is no New York sales tax if you buy a Gold Certificate, but you do attract VAT if you take physical delivery of the underlying gold in London, and you do attract a sales tax in both Zürich and the USA. You don't get clobbered by VAT if you arrange for the gold to be delivered to your bank in the Channel Islands because there is no VAT in these offshore tax havens.

What about a flutter on gold?

You can bet on gold, if you don't want either gold-linked bonds or certificates. For punters who want a flutter on the gold price – either in an upward or downward direction – the IG Index (9–11 Grosvenor Gardens, London SW1, Tel. 01-828 5699) offers the opportunity to bet on gold and a number of other commodities.

Let's take the example of a punter who estimates that the price of gold will go up appreciably. He calls the IG Index and asks for its quotation on one-month gold. For the sake of argument let's suppose that the price of one-month gold in the London bullion market is $607 an ounce. The IG Index quotation to the caller will be $604 to $610 – it makes its 'turn' or profit from the spread between the two prices in the same way that a unit trust makes its turn on the spread between the 'bid' and 'offered' prices on its units. The punter then makes a £10 'up bet' (let's pretend he is calling the IG Index on 3 January) on 5 February gold (one-month gold) at 610. The punter makes £10 for every point by which the closing level of the bet is above 610 or loses £10 for every point by which it is below 610. So, in effect, he has bought gold at 610. Mind you, there are drawbacks because he has to provide a 15 per cent deposit of the overall market value of the gold underlying the bet, therefore, in this case, he has to lodge a deposit of £900 (15 per cent of 610 times £10 = £900).

The punter can close his bet at any stage up to 3.00 pm on the last day of trading (3 February). Let's suppose he decides to let it expire automatically on 3 February. The afternoon London Gold Market price has risen to $713.50 an ounce so that, according to the IG Index, the closing level for the client's bet is 710.

The lucky punter's profit is:

Closing level	710
Opening level	610
Difference	100

The profit on his £10 'up bet' is 100 times £10, or a very useful £1,000. The reverse side of the picture, of course, is that had gold dropped to, say, $513.50 an ounce on that same day his loss would have been calculated on an IG closing level of 510. So the punter's loss would have worked out:

Closing level	510
Opening level	610
Difference	100

His loss on his £10 'up bet' would have been 100 times 10, or £1,000, which would have neatly scooped up his £900 deposit with a further £100 called in to top up.

Let's suppose a punter predicts the price of gold will go down – after all, any gold punter who betted on a fall when gold reached $850 in January 1980 would have reaped rich rewards when the gold price plummetted to under the $500 mark in the following three months. Take the case of a gold punter who wants to make a bet (a 'down bet') that three-month gold will go down.

Let's suppose also that the price of three-month gold in the market is $624.50. The IG Index quotation to the punter is 620 to 629 and the client makes a £250 'down' bet on 5 April gold (three-month gold) at 620. If the gold price falls, he'll make £250 for every point by which the closing level of the bet is below 620, or lose £250 for every point by which it is above 620. In effect he has sold gold at $620. He has to provide a deposit of £23,000 (15 per cent of 620 times £250). He can close his bet at any time over the next three months. He lets it expire automatically on 3 April – and he's been lucky – the London Gold fixing price on the afternoon of the final is $566.6, and so the closing IG Index for the bet is 570. So his profit is:

Opening level	620
Closing level	570
Difference	50

As you can see his profit on a £250 down bet is 50 times £250, or £12,500. Had he been unlucky, and had the gold price risen to the point at which the IG closing level was, say 670, the reverse would have happened and he would have lost 50 times £250, winding up with a loss of £12,500. Bear in mind, if you want to open an account with IG Index (who check out your credit standing with your bankers) the ominous message: 'Please note your risk is not limited to your deposit' is printed in bold type on the application form. Also remember that the spread on a three-month bet, in case you didn't notice it, is higher than the spread on a one-month bet.

The tax on these bets is something of a grey area. One leading tax counsel is of the opinion that IG Index's clients don't have to pay any form of tax if they win. The IG Index itself pays a betting duty on every transaction, so, because the latter takes the form of a bet, theoretically clients pay no income tax, capital gains tax or VAT. I say 'theoretically' because, as with all these grey areas, one never knows if, and when, the Inland Revenue might decide to challenge this tax exemption if a sufficient number of punters were involved and the tax lost to the Inland Revenue was to reach sizeable proportions.

25

Planning ahead – investing for a pension

The complexity of the British State pension scheme is such that the vast majority of those contemplating retirement – without the protection arising from the happy possession of an index-linked pension which is enjoyed by those who retire from the public sector – are probably complacently unaware of the problems they may face.

The theory of the new State pension scheme, which becomes fully operational in 1998, is to eliminate poverty in old age by means of a judicial partnership between the State pension system and private sector occupational pension schemes.

In practice, the new pension scheme (it began in 1978) needs close examination. The new arrangements are formed from three parts. The first part is the 'catch-all' safety net provided by the basic State pension.

The second part is made up by the State earnings-related pension scheme equal to 25 per cent of earnings over an income range of from £29.50 a week to £220 a week, but with a maximum 'ceiling' entitlement of £47.35p a week. To qualify for this you need 20 years of National Insurance contributions which is why the scheme, which started in 1978, becomes fully operational in 1998.

The third part is the 'contracted out' sector. If a private sector employer contracts out of the State scheme, he must provide a company scheme offering retired employees a pension at least as good. The state subsidises these 'guaranteed minimum pensions'. Company schemes offer one-sixtieth (or at least one-eightieth) of final salary for every year of contributions. Many schemes stipulate a maximum pension of two-thirds of final salary.

The problem with the State scheme is that it is looking increasingly doubtful as to whether the State will be able to afford it in 1998. Indeed, the Government actuary has warned that National Insurance contributions will have to rise by at least one-third just to meet the promises of the new system, a rise which would be politically unacceptable. Even if the scheme could fulfil its promises, the earnings-related part of the scheme only looks attractive to the very lowest paid workers – for example, if you earn more than £54 a week the new State pension will not provide you with a 'two-thirds of final salary on retirement' pension.

The answer to the problem – which is why this chapter is included in an 'investment book' – is either to accumulate enough investments from (taxed) income, while working to 'cushion' the retirement years, or to enter into a 'topping up pension scheme' as a supplement to the State scheme and to a company pension scheme.

Controlling directors', or *executive*, pension schemes offer a major extra bonus over and above the self-employed schemes because a company can pay contributions into the scheme out of pre-tax profits. In effect, this means that the Inland Revenue is boosting the pension contributions into a controlling director's pension scheme to the tune of the corporation tax foregone. This major tax boost goes a long way to explaining the boom in controlling directors', or executive, pension schemes over the past couple of decades.

The term 'controlling director' is now interpreted liberally – 'controlling directors' being the back-bone of Britain's small company community, which is 250,000 strong (there are 600,000 limited liability companies of which 250,000 are active). Such a scheme is ideal for the small company community where the business is controlled by a small number of directors. And the benefit of paying premiums from pre-tax profits has not been lost on the medium, and large, companies, many of which have executive pension plans with the large insurance companies.

These are exactly the same in concept as the controlling directors' pension schemes, the idea being to give key executives an extra 'top hat' pension scheme over and above the ordinary company pension scheme, or, if the company is contracted into the State pension scheme, over and above this.

The principle of the controlling directors', or executive, pension schemes is simple enough. An agreement is made to pay in a set amount, such as £500 each year, into the scheme from pre-tax profits. In good years, extra, single premium payments can be paid in, also out of pre-tax profits. The money is accumulated in a fund and invested to boost its growth. Table 24 shows the top three insurance companies in the controlling directors' league over the last 20 years, and the top three over the last 10 years.

The Inland Revenue does impose some restrictions – not on the amount paid in (although it can be unwise to 'overfund' the pension scheme in view of the steady increases in bonus rates), but on the amount taken out. At the end of the day, the Inland Revenue limits the pension to two-thirds of the average of the recipient's last three years of salary, or taxable earnings.

Under Norwich Union's 'Pension Plus Plan' – the top performer over the

Table 24 The top insurance companies in the controlling directors' league

Growth over 20 years (based on £500 invested)*	
Norwich Union	– £500 paid in yearly has grown to £28,714.
Standard Life	– £500 paid in yearly has grown to £28,373.
Scottish Life	– £500 invested has grown to £26,750.
Growth over 10 years (based on £500 invested yearly)	
Equity & Law	– £500 paid in yearly has grown to £11,843.
Equitable Life	– £500 paid in yearly has grown to £11,436.
Standard Life	– £500 paid in yearly has grown to £10,446.

* No return of premium on death.
(Source: *Planned Savings*.)

last 20 years – this would mean the recipient, provided he, or she, has a record of at least ten years' service, would draw a pension of two-thirds of the average earnings in the three years preceding retirement. An average earnings figure of £10,000 would produce a pension of £6,666 and extra 'perks' can be written into the scheme such as the widow's pension entitlement and a yearly escalation scheme (up to the 8¼ per cent escalation maximum is allowed by the Inland Revenue).

Instead of taking the straight pension route, the recipient, after, say, 20 years' service, could take a cash entitlement equal, under the Norwich Union scheme, to one and a half times final salary. The cash released can be used to buy an annuity for the retirement years. Norwich Union's current annuity rates offer, at age 65, £175 yearly for every £1,000 accumulated in the pension scheme.

Self-employed pensions

Many of Britain's two million self-employed – plumbers, electricians, doctors, dentists and a host of others – adopt a somewhat Micawberish principle to their retirement years by making no provision at all, presumably on the principle that, unlike those employed by others who retire at a set age of 60 or 65, the self-employed can soldier on until they drop 'in harness'. Those self-employed people who adopt this somewhat blinkered attitude are missing out on a major tax benefit because their pension contributions attract tax relief at their highest rate of tax. A 60 per cent taxpayer is, in effect, funding his retirement years with almost two-thirds of the cost coming from his, or her, potential tax bill. The Inland Revenue is providing this welcome major boost to the retirement pension while the self-employed are still working. The money paid in premiums during that working life is pooled in an investment fund which pays no tax on its income or capital gains. On retirement, the pension is taxed as earned income, not at the higher, unearned income rate.

There are restrictions as to the level of contributions you can make to a self-employed scheme in any tax year. The limit is 17½ per cent of taxable earnings, but, if you are over 50, you can put in 20 per cent, and the amount you can contribute rises the older you are and the less time you have available to build up a pension scheme. The one problem for the self-employed – who tend to have a much greater freedom of manoeuvre on the tax front than do those in the PAYE net – is that they face a situation in which the more they pay themselves, the more can be paid into a self-employed pension scheme, but the more they pay themselves, the more tax they attract. A 'Catch 22' situation, indeed!

There are two main types of pension schemes open to the self-employed. One is the traditional 'with profits' pension scheme, which offers steady growth and guarantees a basic pension in the retirement years. These schemes are boosted by bonuses each year which, once announced, can not be withdrawn. On retirement, there is a terminal bonus which is an added boost.

The other type of scheme – and currently a major growth sector – is the unit-linked scheme. The money paid into these schemes is then reinvested by the fund's investment managers into ordinary shares (in the United Kingdom and overseas), gilts, property, local authority bonds and a host of other investments. The rationale is that, by adopting a higher risk investment strategy, there is the opportunity of higher rewards, so the investor may not only keep pace with, but also outpace, inflation. The reason why the unit-linked schemes are a major growth sector is because the risk/reward strategy looks attractive to buyers and, more to the point, these schemes are sold directly to the public by marketing-oriented institutions such as Abbey Life and Hambros. The conventional schemes tend to be sold via intermediaries such as insurance brokers who collect return commission for their efforts.

One point of which to beware when you consider unit-linked schemes, whose fortunes are linked with the fortunes of The Stock Exchange and with property, is that if one's retirement year coincides with a general fall back in the investment world (as was the case in 1973 when shares, property and gilts all collapsed), one's retirement pension may be sadly depressed in value, in which case retirement may have to be deferred. Some schemes, such as Norwich Union's 'Pensionvester', offer a switching option into the traditional scheme in the five years preceding retirement. However, during the years you pay into a self-employed unit-linked scheme, you can buy more units when the investment world is sunk in gloom, and the units can be bought cheaply, and you can buy fewer units when the investment world in enjoying one of its periodic bouts of euphoria. To adopt a 'belt and braces approach' you can play safe by switching from a unit-linked scheme, if a switching option is open to you, into the safer haven of a cash deposit scheme wherein the cash is deployed on the money markets, so you know exactly where you stand.

Tables 25 and 26 show the top three performers in the two categories of self-employed pension schemes – the regular, with profit, schemes and the unit-linked schemes. Owing to the more recent introduction of the unit-linked self-employed pension scheme, the tables encompass a ten-year period only. In both cases the 'league tables' — the most recent available – are made up to 1 July 1981.

Table 25 Traditional, with profits, self-employed pension schemes

What a £500 annual premium has grown to over:
20 years
The leaders
Norwich Union – £32,027.
Equitable Life – £31,709.
Prudential – £30,988.
10 years
The leaders
Equitable Life – £10,116.
National Provident Institution – £10,030.
Norwich Union – £9,174.

Table 26 Unit-linked self-employed pension schemes

What a £500 annual premium has grown to over:
10 years
The leaders
M & G (linked with personal pension fund) – £13,352.
Cannon (linked with equity fund) – £11,647.
Save & Prosper (linked with commodity fund) – £11,369.

(Source for both tables: *Planned Savings*.)

Glossary of terms

A Stock Exchange Account A Stock Exchange dealing period which is usually of two weeks, but can be of three. All share purchases and sales which are carried out during the account period are due to be settled on the 'settlement day' relating to that account.

Allotment A term normally used for flotations. It is the number of shares forming part of a new issue allotted to the new issue applicant. The allotment letter is the document which provides the investor with evidence of his allotment and is of obvious interest if cash borrowed from the bank is being used to stay an issue.

Authorized capital The maximum number of shares which can be issued by a company without the prior approval of shareholders. This can be the same as the total shares in issue, or may well be more than the shares in issue.

Averaging When a share drops in price, some investors follow the technique of 'averaging'. This involves buying more shares at the lower price and thus 'averaging down' the cost. The same holds true of shares rising in price when further purchases are made.

Balance certificate A certificate representing the balance of shares due back to the seller after only part of the shareholding is sold.

Bear An investor who sells shares he doesn't own in the belief that the shares will fall. If he does not own the shares he is selling, he is in an exposed position because he has to deliver the shares by the due date after the sale takes place.

Covered bear Someone who sells shares *he already owns* in the expectation that the share price will fall and he can complete the transaction *without risk*.

Bear market A period when all share prices fall 'across the board' on the stock market. When shares rise across the board, this is referred to as a *bull market* – although many commentators hedge their bets on both bear and bull markets by referring to them as 'technical corrections'.

Bearer security A stock which passes to another buyer without any formality in the transferring process. United Kingdom shares are all registered in the name of the buyer. Eurobonds, however, are virtually all bearer securities, providing complete anonymity (if bought by way of an overseas bank account).

Bed and breakfasting The old practice of selling a share one day, towards the end of the tax year, in order to establish a capital gain/loss, and buying it back the next. Now more sophisticated techniques must be used.

Dealing 'at best' If you tell your broker to 'buy at best' this means you are willing to buy a share *without a limit on the price*. The alternative is to set a price limit on the purchase *at the risk of not being able to buy any shares at all*. The same process applies to selling shares.

Best terms You pay broker's commission on terms which do not involve the broker sharing with an agent. When you buy through your bank, or another intermediary such as an accountant, they will probably be registered as agents to The Stock Exchange.

Bid The jobber in a share 'bids' for a share. The jobber doesn't know whether your broker's 'man in the market' is approaching him as a buyer or seller, and therefore he will quote a 'spread' for a share which can be a couple of pence on a popular, heavily traded share, or 10p, 20p, or even more, on a share which does not figure prominently on his 'book' of shares.

Blue chips The ordinary shares of big companies (such as ICI or Marks & Spencer) whose ability to continue making profits and paying a dividend is beyond question.

Bonus issue A company decides to increase its share capital by converting its reserves (a surplus on revaluation of property, for example) into shares which are distributed free to existing shareholders. Other terms used for this are a *scrip issue* or a *capitalisation issue*.

Jobber's book The day-by-day record of shares bought and sold by a jobber.

Call The payment of all, or part, of the issue price of shares which were originally issued 'nil paid' or on a 'partly paid' basis.

Capital distribution The distribution of money to shareholders out of capital rather than trading profits – for example if a company sells off land and buildings surplus to requirements. A capital distribution can be caried out if the nominal value of the capital is reduced and the surplus thrown up is distributed to shareholders.

Capital 'gains tax' (CGT) A tax on profits on, for example, share dealing.

Capital 'transfer tax' A cumulative tax applied to gifts made during a lifetime – including gifts of shares or gilts – and on the assets left after death.

Cash settlement Settlement in cash for the purchase and sale of shares, etc., normally the day after the transaction is carried out. For example, if you deal in the traded options market, settlement has to be for cash whereas, in normal share dealing, settlement is delayed to the appropriate Stock Exchange account's settlement day.

Clean The price of a share or gilt after allowing for any dividend or accrued interest which is reflected in the market-place.

Closing prices The prices ruling at the official close of The Stock Exchange at 3.30 p.m. Bear in mind that professionals in the market can deal before 10 a.m. and after 3.30 p.m. (the official dealing hours).

Convertible A loan stock, share, or gilt, with rights to transfer into another security at a predetermined price at a predetermined date in the future.

Corporation tax The tax chargeable on all the profits of a company. There are a number of well known corporation tax mitigation devices such as leasing which can reduce, or eliminate, corporation tax liability.

Coupon A voucher attached to a bearer security which entitles you to collect dividends or interest payments. Vouchers on Eurobonds are prime favourites for 'black economy operators' who can cash them at any bank branch of most airports, gross of tax.

Cover The earnings available to cover the dividend payment after meeting other charges such as preference share coupons or bank interest payments.

Cum 'Cum' is used to describe an investment which is bought with extra bonuses accruing, such as a dividend in the case of a share. 'Ex' means just the opposite – for example 'ex-rights'.

Deferred shares A class of shares which ranks after the ordinary shares because it may have no voting rights attached. These are sometimes described as 'A' shares and are not popular with The Stock Exchange Council.

Dividend The income declared payable on a shareholding. The dividend voucher is the form which accompanies the dividend payment and is proof of tax paid to the Inland Revenue. The dividend warrant is a form of cheque used for payment of dividends.

Dividend yield The annual gross of tax dividend per share as a percentage of the share price.

Earnings per share The net profits of a company available for ordinary shareholders. This can be paid as a dividend, retained within the company, or both. The earnings yield is the annual earnings per share as a percentage of the share price.

Fixed assets The land, buildings, plant and machinery which are a permanent part of a company's assets, over which a bank can take a 'fixed' charge. This type of asset can be contrasted with the floating assets over which a bank can take a 'floating' charge.

Front-end loading The charges payable at the outset, for example, buying units in a unit trust involves a front-end loading of around 5½ per cent.

Gearing The relationship of debt to equity. In a lending banker's eyes a gearing ratio of 30 per cent would be reasonable. The ratio differs with the nature of the business – you could expect a property company to have a high gearing ratio of, say, 60 per cent.

Gilt edged The stock issued by the British Government borrowing via the market. Theoretically the Government, which can levy taxes on all its residents, should be the last to go bust in a general financial collapse – hence the term 'good as gilts'.

'In house' fund A fund managed by a stockbroking firm rather than a unit trust. It is used for small clients of the stockbroker concerned.

Insider dealing Buying or selling shares on the basis of privileged information unknown to the market – now a criminal offence under the Companies Act 1980.

Interim report A statement of company profits (normally after six months) for any period less than a trading period (normally a year).

Introduction One method of going public – no formal sale of shares is involved as the shares are 'introduced' to the market.

Issued capital The amount of the authorised share capital of a company which has been issued on the market.

Jobber A member of The Stock Exchange who deals in stocks and shares on his own account, and only with brokers and other jobbers.

Licensed dealer A dealer in securities licensed under the provision of the Prevention of Frauds (Investments) Act.

Limit A price given to a broker above which, or below which, he is not allowed to buy, or sell, shares.

Limited liability The liability of shareholders for the debts of a company is limited to the value of their nominal shareholding.

Liquidation A company can be wound up via a liquidation and the creditors get paid according to their priority (the shareholders are paid last). It can also apply to a reduction in the number of units in issue in a unit trust.

Market capitalisation The value at the current market price of all the ordinary shares of a company.

Marking The price at which a bargain is struck in the stock market and which appears, for example, in the *Financial Times* on a Saturday.

Middle price The price midway between the bid, and offer, prices quoted by a jobber for a share.

Net asset value The net asset value per share is the total of all the company's assets (which are due to the ordinary shareholders) less the borrowings and other prior charges. If the market price is less than the net asset value (nav) per share, it can be described as being 'at a discount'. If it is over the net asset value per share, it is described as being 'at a premium'. The figure of nav is arrived at by dividing the net value of the assets by the number of shares in issue (normally the number of ordinary, or equity, shares in issue).

Nil paid A new issue, usually a rights issue, on which no payment is called for initially.

Offer price The price at which a jobber will sell shares.

Offer for sale The most popular method for a new issue.

Offshore fund An investment fund located in the Channel Islands or Isle of Man. Most commodity funds are 'off-shore'.

Paid up The amount of 'calls' paid on partly-paid shares.

Placing Another method of going public – a line of shares placed directly by the selling brokers with institutional investors without going through the market.

Preference share A share with a fixed coupon attached to it which ranks ahead of ordinary shares in the event of a receivership.

Price/earnings ratio The ratio of a share price to earnings per share.

Prospectus The document giving details of a company going public.

Quotation The acceptance of a share by The Stock Exchange, permitting dealing to be carried out in that share.

Renunciation Giving up your right to be registered as the holder of a new issue so that it can be transferred to another investor.

Settlement/account day The day appointed for the settlement of transactions carried out in an account. This is on a Monday, ten days after the end of each account.

Stag An investor who applies for more shares in a new issue than he can afford to buy, in the hope of getting an allotment letter which can be sold at a profit on first day's dealings.

Stop-loss order An order to a broker to sell a share immediately should the price drop to a specified level.

Tender Another method of going public under which shares are offered to the highest bidder. Normally the price is set by the institutional investment managers leaving small applicants to write 'striking price' on the application form.

Warrant The right to subscribe for shares at some time in the future. The warrant can be bought and sold in the market.

Index